CW00872025

Endorsements

Harold Reed has provided a well-researched and thoughtful description of both the types of healthcare professionals and the community support that is necessary to sustain a healthcare infrastructure in rural Alabama. He brings to life the compassion and dedication of all involved. You can feel Harold's own commitment and dedication to quality healthcare as he narrates this history.

Mike Horsley, President
Alabama Hospital Association

"Harold Reed, an outstanding rural health administrator and now author, does an exceptional job of describing the evolution of medical service in Fayette County and documenting the many contributions that local practitioners have made to health care in the county, Alabama, and even the world. His detailed research and description of the county's health care heroes prompts thoughts concerning the future of health care and an anticipation and confidence that Fayette County practitioners will be heavily involved in this determination."

Dale E. Quinney, Executive Director
Alabama Rural Health Association

Mr. Reed's treatise on medical care in Fayette County provides a retrospective review of the development of a healthcare system in one rural Alabama county. In that retrospective, one sees not only the transformation of healthcare over the past century in Fayette County but also a pattern that has, no doubt, been replicated in dozens of other counties in Alabama and probably in hundreds across our nation. He has captured the visionaries, the builders, and the leaders who, through their dedication, have contributed so much to healthcare in Fayette County. Mr. Reed's narrative not only captures the facts, but also humanizes the past with anecdotes, which help better define the picture he has drawn. With 38 years of service to Fayette Medical Center, Mr. Reed is well placed to tell this story with detail and passion

Donald E. Williamson, M.D.
State Health Officer
State of Alabama

Fayette County Medicine: A History of Quality Health Care in Rural Alabama is a fun read, and not only for locals who will want to read it to bask in nostalgia and their collective memories of the county, but for anyone serious about understanding rural medicine and its impact on and importance to communities. From the documentation of the commitment of these dedicated health professionals ("Dr. McNease was so busy with his practice that his daughter, Pat McCrackin ... said that she once went three weeks without seeing her father. "He was gone in the mornings before I got up and he came home after I was asleep"), to a look at the many roles rural doctors found themselves fulfilling ("[Dr. Sanford] once baptized a patient... in the whirlpool at the hospital"), to a worrisome glimpse at today's struggle to maintain the services so vital for these communities ("The survival of individual doctors' practices and of rural hospitals is at stake."), health professionals, policy makers, and civic leaders would be well advised to study this story of Fayette County.

Richard H. Streiffer, MD
Dean and Professor of Family Medicine
College of Community Health Sciences
University of Alabama

"If you like history then you will find this historical overview of the way rural medicine and healthcare developed in Fayette County since the early 1800's absolutely fascinating. Harold Reed gives a detailed account of the men and women who laid the groundwork for modern medicine. Reed provides this historical overview as one who not only knows healthcare but who knows the area firsthand as he has dedicated his life to the wellbeing of others in the very area he writes about."

-Robert Aderholt
U.S. House of Representatives
Alabama

FAYETTE COUNTY MEDICINE:
A History
of
Quality Health Care
in Rural Alabama

Harold Reed

Edited by
John R. Wheat

FAYETTE COUNTY MEDICINE:
A History
of
Quality Health Care
in Rural Alabama

Quality, The Physicians, The
McNease-Robertson-Hodo Clinic/
Hospital and their Legacy

Harold Reed

With Foreword by John R. Wheat, MD
and
Epilogue by William A. Curry, MD

Copy Editor Pat Norton
Contributing Editor R. O. Rutland, MD
Assisting Editor Delbert Reed
Editor John R Wheat, MD

ISBN: 978-1-4834-1582-6 (hc)
ISBN: 978-1-4834-1583-3 (e)

Lulu Publishing Services rev. date: 08/15/2014

Contents

Foreword by John R. Wheat, MD, MPH

Perhaps as only a lifelong resident of a rural community can, Harold Reed has captured the insider's view of health care as it evolved in Fayette County, Alabama. Even better, he has lived much of this history as his own career in health care progressively climbed and peaked along with Fayette's medical community. He was there in a most personal way to benefit by the advances in medical education, technology, and the health care system that saved his life and in so doing preserved this remarkable history. It is a labor of love, perhaps even some hero worship, but it is more than a personal reminiscence; it has a scholarly bent. It is obvious that much research has been done to exact historical facts as far as possible, and at least a yeoman's effort has been made to place these facts in some order and in a broader context.

John R. Wheat, MD, MPH is Professor of Community and Rural Medicine in the College of Community Health Sciences at The University of Alabama.

This historical narrative is remarkable for its view of health care from the countryside. Too often the story of human advancement is told from an urban or academic vantage point. In such cases, little is learned about the influence of the indigenous on societal developments. That story often tells of the shortcomings of rural health care and the virtues of urban outreach. This book is a rare look at history from the other side. We see where Fayette, Alabama, a small rural community, has valued modern medical care at every bend in the path of its history. We see leadership exerted by the men, and later the women, of medicine to set the course and the efforts of others to sustain the high ideals and maintain the direction. We see adaptations made to accommodate evolving policies and economic threats. We see through Harold Reed's eyes the gradual assembling of a network of relationships among physicians, staff, administrators, community, medical education institutions, and tertiary medical systems to provide the elasticity to bend and bow with the times, but to survive and sustain the quality of care expected.

As Reed tells about each physician, we begin to see some patterns. Most of the physicians have small town or rural roots. Many grew up in or around the Fayette area. Harold Reed puts flesh on the bare bones of health workforce research that finds "rural background" to be an important factor in the production of rural physicians. There are some familiar stereotypes found in this history--the faithful, overworked country doctor. Who could forget the anecdote shared of Dr. McNease establishing a special private place in town to park his car and catch a nap after the exhaustion of a day in the office and an evening on the back roads, but still be centrally available in case of sudden need? But perhaps surprising is the little heard story of how rural family physicians have had major impact on the development of medical education and on state professional associations. This is best exemplified by Dr. Rutland's key role in starting a medical school and residency training program at The University of Alabama, but also highlighted in Dr. John Morrison's unbending commitment to scholarship with surgery that reached world-wide acclaim and landed him in a major state medical school to share his science and art with the next generation of surgeons.

Finally, there is something fresh in the way that Harold Reed portrays his colleagues and neighbors; after all, in a small town all are neighbors, as one can see in this narrative. We see physicians, nurses, administrators, and technical and support staff as people who are not only engaged in their craft, but also in the community. These are people who identify with their community and expect the best for it, for the sake of their families and their neighbors. They are involved in health care, but also in the life of the community through civic organizations, religious affiliations, and public service.

For all these reasons, this book makes a contribution to the understanding of rural health care--where it has arrived and how it got here--that is missed by most histories of medicine. Besides that, it is a fun read.

Dedication

This book is dedicated to the physicians and health care workers, both those named in this book and those unnamed, whose passion for their professions and commitment to the community led them to provide the highest quality health care possible to the people of Fayette County and surrounding areas.

Preface

There have been constant improvements in the quality of health care worldwide over the last two centuries. These changes are documented typically through advances in urban and academic medical practice. Health care in rural places has not had the same public exposure, which might leave an impression that modern health care should not be expected to be found outside the city. However, this is not necessarily the case, as demonstrated in the remarkable efforts of health professionals down through the years in Fayette County, Alabama. The Fayette County medical community has a tradition of keeping up with the times.

Alabama was populated by Native Americans, then French and Spanish coming from the Gulf of Mexico, and then by British and Americans filtering in from the North and East. Africans made a major contribution to opening this fertile new territory to agricultural production. Population shifts are accompanied by conflict, economic turmoil, and diseases. Alabama witnessed its share of these miseries with battles and wars, abject poverty, and, always, illness. Malaria, yellow fever, pellagra, and hookworms are but the most visible of the epidemics to plague the early settlers of Alabama. Life in these early years was a risky proposition due to hazardous occupations, infant deaths, maternal difficulty with childbirth, infectious diseases, and the scarcity of physicians.

Alabama became a state on December 14, 1819. Five years later, Fayette County was formed. The "old Southwest" of Alabama and Mississippi was still being transformed from Native American to a European American and African American territory, attracting the farmers and plantation owners, land speculators, lawyers, storekeepers, physicians, and others who would take the early risks that opened this region to modernization. As Alabama began to grow as a state, Fayette County kept pace, and its medical community proved to be at the forefront of local developments.

In the 1800s, the irregular, unregulated practice of medicine flourished everywhere. Estimates have shown that, in the early days of Alabama as a state, the number of irregular practitioners far exceeded the number of qualified physicians. There were German root doctors, homoeopathists, steam doctors, and black faith doctors as late as 1859. Health care in the late 1800s and the early part of the 1900s was provided mostly by country doctors who had little or no formal training. If a young man wanted to practice medicine, he would simply become an apprentice to an established doctor and, after several years of training, hang up his own shingle. In addition to these doctors, many illnesses and disorders were treated by midwives, family remedies, and local druggists (Howard L. Holley, MD, *A History of Medicine in Alabama*, 1997.)

Dr. Reuben Davis was one such doctor who trained

as an apprentice. When he was 16 years old he moved to Monroe County, Mississippi to live with his sister and to apprentice with her husband, Dr. George Higgason. Reuben received his training by studying with Dr. Higgason and accompanying him on his visits to the sick. Much of their time, day and night, was spent in the saddle.

On December 24, 1828, Dr. Reuben Davis arrived in the small, struggling town of Fayette Court House (the name of Fayette at that time) in Fayette County. He must be considered a good doctor for his time because of his preference for using Peruvian bark (made into a drug by Jesuit priests) and whiskey rather than purgatives and bleeding of patients, which were in vogue. In 1829, Dr. Davis married Mary Halbeert. And demonstrating the relative status of medicine at the time, he soon became interested in law, and in 1832 he and his wife left Fayette for Mississippi, where he became a leading lawyer of the state. When the Civil War came, he was a member of the Confederate Congress in Richmond, Virginia. He was known as a good lawyer and statesman. When he was a doctor in Fayette, he had a good practice and might have stayed, had his income not been so small. When he left for Mississippi, he had three dollars in his pocket.

Later, Fayette County had doctors with at least some formal training, for which they were considered pioneers. Dr. A. Lanthus Blakeney (1883-1959) came from a farming family and was a life-long resident of Newtonville, Alabama, in southern Fayette County. He graduated from Grant Medical College in Chattanooga, Tennessee in 1907 and immediately thereafter practiced one year in the Moore's Bridge Community in northern Tuscaloosa County. In 1908, he purchased the practice of W. W. Jones in nearby Newtonville. He married the former Velma Davis (1886-1984) of Kennedy, Alabama that same year, and they had one son, Adolph. (Velma was the aunt of Dr. William Davis who currently has a practice in Vernon, Alabama and had admitting

Dr. Blakeney, Velma and Adolph

privileges at Fayette Medical Center until he chose to stop admitting.) Dr. Blakeney practiced medicine in Newtonville for 51years with the assistance of his wife. Dr. Blakeney was civic minded and was a deacon in the Shepherd Baptist Church.

Other practitioners in Fayette in the early 1900s included brothers Dr. J. A. Brandon and Dr. A. C. Brandon, Dr. A. J. Stewart, Dr. D. H. Wright, and Dr. J. D. Young. Their names are familiar because some of them still have relatives living in Fayette County. Dr. J. A. Brandon's wife was named Edna. Horace and Harold Berry are their grandsons. Dr. A. C. Brandon was Jim Walker Brandon's grandfather. However, little information is available about these men. For example, their education and years of practice were not available publicly. There were others whose names have been forgotten.

Dr. Richard Carter practiced in Fayette around the late 1940s and early 1950s. Dr. Carter received his Doctor of Medicine from Tulane and, after a tour of duty in the Army, came to Fayette to practice until he could make enough money to complete a residency program in internal medicine, which he did in Birmingham. After he completed the residency program, Dr. Carter taught at the University of Alabama School of Medicine in Birmingham for a short time. However, he served for most of his medical career with the Disability Determination Service in Birmingham, where, coincidentally, he worked with Andy Shelton whom he had delivered while practicing in Fayette.

Medical education and medicine in the United States took a major turn toward science a decade into the Twentieth Century. The vast majority of medical schools of the day were privately owned by one or more doctors, and these were closed as a result of the Flexner Report, which favored medical schools as official components of universities and affiliated with hospitals. In Alabama, as in the rest of the country, medical education was being re-designed based on the "German model," best exemplified in the United States by Johns Hopkins University.

Perhaps this overhaul of medical education accounts, in part, for the tremendous change in the quality of health services in the small rural community of Fayette, Alabama, when Benjamin Wilberne McNease, MD arrived in 1926. Dr. McNease has been called the father of modern medicine in Fayette County, and he was said by some to be the first doctor in Fayette to be trained in a formal medical school in a scientific manner. He had five years of formal medical training, which for that time was well above average. Proverbs 29:18 says, "Where there is no vision the people perish," and Dr. McNease brought both the vision and determination to improve the quality of health care in Fayette County, a task for which he was well prepared by his training.

Dr. McNease was followed to Fayette County by many other excellently trained doctors who also were determined to practice through trying circumstances that have affected Fayette along with other rural communities throughout the South. The economic ups and downs of agriculture and light manufacturing are perhaps uppermost in these stresses. Some physicians stayed for their entire careers, while others practiced in Fayette for only a short while before moving on. But each contributed to the continual improvement in the quality of health care in Fayette County. The people of Fayette County have been extremely fortunate over the years to have physicians who brought with them the benefits of a modern medical education.

As medicine and health care have become more complicated, the quality of care has come to depend increasingly on other employees and health professionals, in addition to doctors. Long term observers of Fayette's medical care system agree that employees in this growing health care profession have made major contributions and have assisted the doctors in every way possible. In the early years, doctors trained their own employees in the skills that were needed. The doctors and their assistants worked long hours under difficult circumstances without complaint. In those early years, there was a camaraderie and sense of family among those involved in the struggle against illness and disease. As we survey the uncertain status of health care in many rural communities throughout Alabama and the nation today, all the doctors and health care workers who worked to establish Fayette's remarkable health care system are to be commended for their noble efforts. However, it is to Dr. B. W. McNease that we attribute the new and more modern approach to quality health care in Fayette County. He demonstrated that quality health care could be provided in a small community.

Benjamin Wilberne McNease, MD

General Practice

Dr. Benjamin Wilberne McNease was born on July 9, 1897, and raised in the small southeastern town of Carson, Mississippi. He attended the University of Mississippi for

his undergraduate degree and was an outstanding player on the Ole Miss baseball team. He developed a life-long affection for Ole Miss athletics and often returned to Oxford for football games. Dr. McNease stayed at Ole Miss after college and completed the first two, or pre-clinical, years, of medical school. He then

Benjamin W. McNease, M.D.

attended the University of Pennsylvania for his last two clinical years and received the Doctor of Medicine degree. He returned to the South for his internship at the Tennessee Coal and Iron (TCI) Hospital, later known as the Lloyd Noland Hospital, in Fairfield, Alabama. It was there that he met his loving wife Alma, who worked as a dietitian at TCI and later worked as a dietitian with the McNease-Robertson Hospital in Fayette. Dr. McNease depended on Alma for her steadfast support, personally and professionally.

Dr. McNease was considered a quick learner and a bright young man who enjoyed teaching. His interest in teaching carried over into Fayette when for several years Fayette served as a family practice preceptorship site for the University of Alabama School of Medicine in Birmingham, Alabama.

When Dr. McNease completed his year of internship at TCI, he took a teaching position at the University of Alabama School of Medicine, which was in Tuscaloosa at that time and provided the pre-clinical years of medical school. The school had an outstanding reputation for scientific-based training. Dr. McNease became known as an excellent instructor

B.W. McNease, Medical School

in several subjects, but he was best known for his classes in human anatomy. Through his training and academic work, he established contact with many other highly regarded doctors around the country with whom he could consult. At about this time, Joe Posey Robertson, plant manager for Brown Lumber Company in Fayette, recognized the need for a well-qualified doctor in the area. He became aware of Dr. McNease and worked diligently and successfully to recruit Dr. McNease to Fayette. Dr. McNease arrived in Fayette on June 24, 1926, as the company doctor for Brown Lumber Company and soon became very busy with his own practice. He was reported to be the first doctor in Fayette to be trained in a formal, scientific manner; but if he was not the first, he was certainly the first to have the passion to start the tradition of quality health care that has been passed down from generation to generation. Dr. McNease was the father of modern medicine in Fayette County. He endured many difficulties in his quest to

B.W. McNease, M.D.

improve the health care of Fayette County and dedicated his life to his profession. One difficulty Dr. McNease had to endure was the lack of paved roads in Fayette County, and he made house calls all over the county. The first paved road in Fayette County was Temple Avenue. It was paved from the depot to the first intersection beyond the First Baptist Church in 1926, the same year Dr. McNease came to Fayette.

On the first day that Dr. McNease saw patients in Fayette, T. H. Robertson, president of Citizens Bank of Fayette, had a motorcycle accident and became one of Dr. McNease's first patients. Robertson was seriously injured, but was well cared for. The paths of these two community leaders crossed again shortly thereafter when Dr. McNease needed financial assistance in building a clinic and hospital.

Dr. McNease brought with him his knowledge of modern medicine. The community appreciated the standards he set in high quality and compassionate health care that he provided. He had a clear vision of how health care services should and could be improved and expanded to better serve the area.

From the very beginning, Dr. McNease was so busy that it was not unusual for him to see 40 patients a day in his office, then leave for house calls. He soon knew every country road in Fayette County, and after working long hours he could fall asleep anywhere. Dr. McNease had a few places where he could stop and get a quick nap when he was out making house calls. One place he especially liked was behind Mr. Thomas Lindsey's home, which was centrally located near the First Methodist Church. He could pull his car around back of Mr. Lindsey's house where he knew no one could see him and he would not be disturbed.

Probably one of the most trying times for Dr. McNease in his early years in Fayette came during the flu epidemic in 1929. During that time, he and his wife Alma often took into their home the care of 20 to 30 patients, while also continuing his office practice. To make things even more difficult, the Great Depression was starting during 1929-30. Penicillin had been discovered by Alexander Fleming in 1928 and would have been of great help at that time in Fayette, but it did not become available until many years later.

Dr. McNease had a heavy workload, but he saw the value in being involved in organized medicine, also. He was once president of the Medical Association of the State of Alabama, chairman of the State Board of Censors, and chairman of the State Board of Health. He was also a delegate to the American Medical Association.

Dr. McNease was so busy with his practice that his daughter, Pat McCrackin, who became a pharmacist, said that she once went three weeks without seeing her father. "He was gone in the mornings before I got up and he came home after I was asleep," she said.

Dr. Henry Hodo, in reference to Dr. McNease, quoted Ben Franklin as saying, "In darkness as in light our responsibilities are with us." Then he said, "It was this sense of duty and responsibility for the health care of the people of this area that prompted Dr. B. W. McNease to build a clinic and a hospital."

Dr. McNease saw a great need for a modern clinic to expand his ability to meet the needs of the area, and in April of 1936 he purchased for $500 a small piece of property on which to build a clinic. The site was a perfect place for a clinic. It was downtown in a convenient location and had a beautiful, large oak tree that stood at the rear of the clinic. This oak tree was over 100 years old and was later marked with a plaque as a "Champion Tree" by the Alabama Forestry Commission for being the largest of its species in Alabama.

The Citizens Bank of Fayette saw tremendous value

in lending the money to construct a modern clinic in Fayette. However, such a loan was considered a high risk during the poor economy, and banker Robertson thought that the bank examiners would question it. To prevent any possible issues, Robertson moved the loan from the bank to his store, the T. H. Robertson and Son General Mercantile store, where the loan would not be subject to review by bank auditors. The Robertson and Son store was very large and was located on the city block behind where the bank is located currently.

The McNease Clinic was completed in 1937 for a cost of $11,000. It featured 12 examination rooms, a modern x-ray machine, a sun lamp, ultraviolet rays, and other equipment representing the latest technology. Dr. McNease, with his new, modern clinic, offered a wide range of health care services to his patients. Many locals believe that Dr. McNease would not have started construction of his clinic-hospital unless he had known that Dr. Banks Robertson, a general surgeon, was coming to Fayette after completing his general surgery residency. Dr. Robertson did come to Fayette and had a very busy and successful practice.

Immediately after construction of the clinic was complete, construction of the adjoining McNease-Robertson Hospital was started. The hospital made it possible to admit patients and to perform surgery locally. Prior to the hospital being built, it was not unusual for Dr. McNease to place a patient in a hotel room to give him fluids, because the nearest hospital was in Jasper or Tuscaloosa. Sometimes, for seriously ill patients, Dr.

McNease would ride the train with them to Jasper to be admitted. The modernized McNease-Robertson Hospital, when completed, had a bed capacity for 17 patients. It was later expanded to hold 21 patients. Room rates were five dollars per day for a private room and three dollars per day for ward beds.

The hospital was staffed only by nurses who were graduates of a three-year Nursing program. For living quarters, the nurses had a house just to the rear of the hospital. At that time, in the Fayette area, the only practical options for a hospital stay were in Jasper, Tuscaloosa, or Fayette. The facility was costly to operate, but Dr. McNease and Dr. Robertson focused more on their patients' health care needs than on their ability to pay.

Dr. McNease and Dr. Robertson continued to operate the clinic-hospital throughout World War II (1939-45). Dr. McNease was 43 years old when the war started, too old to be drafted into military service. However, he served his country at home as physician and as chairman of the local Selective Services Board. If he had tried to join, he probably would have been sent home due to his critically important role as doctor in the community. During the war, his practice was extremely busy—he is quoted as saying, "If there is another war I sure as hell will volunteer before I will stay here and work like this."

Because of years of uncompensated, patriotic service to the nation on the Selective Services Board, Dr. McNease received certificates of appreciation from four different presidents of the United States. The certificates were signed also by the governors of Alabama. These certificates are on display by the Fayette Historical Society at the Fayette Depot. The signing officials were as follows:

Governors of Alabama	Presidents of the United States
Chauncey Sparks	Franklin D. Roosevelt
Jim Folsom	Harry Truman
Gordon Persons	Dwight Eisenhower
John Patterson	John F. Kennedy

Dr. McNease was sometimes accused of being rough with his patients, which was attributed to his having a large patient load and not enough time. He certainly was a compassionate man with a big heart and at times demonstrated quite a sense of humor. In one instance, Dr. McNease walked into the exam room to see a small boy with his mother. The young boy had cut his knee on a broken soft drink bottle and the wound needed several stitches. The boy was on the verge of tears, when Dr. McNease looked at the chart and said in his deep voice, "Young man, did you know you and I are the same age? My birthday is July tenth just like yours." The boy made no comment but had a sheepish grin. Dr. McNease continued to care for the boy, and the boy remained calm throughout the procedure.

Benjamin Wilburn McNease, MD, was a dominant figure in medicine for 46 years in Fayette County. He operated the only clinic-hospital in Fayette County for 21 years, and his name remains associated with the highest quality of health care. Dr. McNease was very busy, but he was also involved in the community and never neglected his family or his church. He was a man of firm resolve, but he also had a compassionate heart and cared greatly for his family, his community, and his fellow man. He was also instrumental in bringing into Fayette young doctors who shared his concern for high quality health care services.

John Banks Robertson, Sr., MD

General Surgery

Dr. John Banks Robertson, Sr. was a man with great passion for everything he undertook. He grew up in Lamar County, adjacent to Fayette County, in Vernon, Alabama and was a bright student and outstanding athlete. He was a star running back for the Vernon High School football team and received a full scholarship to The University of Alabama to play football. However, in his sophomore year he

John Banks Robertson, Sr., MD

injured his right knee and was unable to continue to play. He gave up his scholarship and worked at various jobs to continue his studies at the University. Dr. Robertson was friends with Alabama football alumnus Bill "Swamp" Sanders, a Fayette native who might well have had some influence on Dr. Robertson later locating his medical practice in Fayette.

Dr. Robertson completed his undergraduate degree and the two pre-clinical years of medical school at The

University of Alabama, which did not yet have the clinical years. From there he went to Tulane University School of Medicine for his two clinical years, and in 1934 he received the Doctor of Medicine degree. He then went to Hillman Hospital in Birmingham, where he completed his intern year on June 30, 1935, and two years of surgery residency in June 1937.

As an intern at Hillman Hospital, Dr. Robertson was given room, board, laundry, and whites, as scrubs were called at that time. He was paid ten dollars per month, five dollars of which he sent home to assist his parents. Hillman Hospital had an outstanding reputation as a teaching hospital and Dr. Robertson said, "Hillman was one of the best training facilities in the country." Later, other Fayette physicians including Doctors Henry Hodo, Inez Fowler, and Richard Rutland received some training at Hillman Hospital prior to coming to Fayette.

Dr. John B. Robertson, Sr.

The history of Hillman began around 1870 when several attempts were made to organize a hospital for the indigent in Birmingham. The Society of the United Charities was organized in January of 1884 and resolved to build and maintain such a hospital. After many years of financial difficulties, being destroyed by fire, relocating and rebuilding, having changes in ownership, and enduring disasters, it continued to survive. In 1940, the 575-bed Jefferson Hospital was built adjacent to the Hillman Hospital and together they became known as the Jefferson-Hillman Hospital. In 1943, the question arose as to where to locate a proposed University of Alabama four-year medical school. On December 20, 1944, the Jefferson-Hillman hospital was given outright to The University of Alabama. The four-year Medical College of Alabama became a reality in 1945 when the University of Alabama two-year School of Medicine moved from Tuscaloosa to the Jefferson-Hillman Hospital in Birmingham. Jefferson-Hillman was renamed the University of Alabama Hospital and Hillman Clinics in 1955, and in 1965 it became the University of Alabama Hospitals and Clinics. Today it is named UAB Hospital as part of the University of Alabama at Birmingham and is owned by the State of Alabama.

During Dr. Robertson's last year at Hillman Hospital, he was named chief resident. Chief residents at that time were responsible for more than just their sub-specialty; they were chief resident of all services. Dr. Robertson's abilities were not only noted by his being named chief resident, but also by his being a board-certified member of the American College of Surgeons. At the time he completed his residency in June of 1937, it was a difficult time to start a practice. Everyone was trying to recover from the Great Depression of 1929–30, and Germany had invaded Poland on September 1, 1936, to start World War II. These difficulties didn't deter Dr. Robertson, however, because he had great respect for Dr. McNease and shared a vision with him for the provision of quality health care in and around Fayette County. Dr. Robertson was anxious to locate his practice in Fayette because it was close to his family in Vernon and he had a strong desire to help patients of all socioeconomic levels in the area.

Dr. McNease constructed his clinic the same year Dr. Robertson started his practice in Fayette. It had the best of everything for its day. As soon as the clinic was complete, construction of the adjoining hospital was begun. Because of its modern equipment, the doctors were able to provide a wide range of services to their patients. Dr. Robertson realized those were difficult times for his patients; his son, John Banks Robertson, Jr., stated that his father told him that he never charged as much as $100 for any surgery except for two extremely difficult cases. Dr. Robertson worked very long hours and even lived in the back of the hospital during the first few years of his practice. After a long normal day in surgery and seeing patients in the clinic, Dr. Robertson and Dr. McNease would divide the county in half and make house calls until late into the night. Either before or after house calls,

Dr. Robertson would make evening rounds in the hospital.

After arriving in Fayette, Dr. Robertson met and married his wife, Ms. Jeff Richards. Dr. Robertson was a loving husband and father and his wife was constantly at his side, supporting him in every way possible. Quite interestingly, Ms. Richards came from a highly motivated and successful family. Her father, Mr. A.J. Richards, was a successful businessman in Fayette. He owned and operated several businesses including the power company, which supplied electrical power to the city. Mr. Richards also built the first movie theater in Fayette, which was run later by his daughter, Lucile Cobb, and grandson, R. C. Cobb. They built a theater of their own in Fayette on the corner of the courthouse lawn and named it the Richards Theater after Mr. Richards. This theater business grew from its small beginnings in Fayette to what is today the widely known Cobb Theaters.

Another of Mr. Richards' daughters was nicknamed "Temp." She married Don Hutson, a famous football player at The University of Alabama. He played at the same time as Paul "Bear" Brant, both playing at the end position. However, Don was so good that Bear Bryant referred to himself as the "other end." Don was an All-American while at Alabama and later played for the Green Bay Packers for 11 years, 10 of which he was All Pro.

Wiley Clemons, one of the hospital's male employees, was a great asset to Dr. Robertson, who trained Wiley to be an excellent assistant. Wiley could put on casts, insert catheters, and do anything else Dr. Robertson trained him to do. It was said that Dr. Robertson had to show Wiley only one time and he would be able to carry out the task from then on. In addition to helping patients, Wiley had his share of housekeeping and maintenance work to attend to. Wiley was also a great help to Dr. McNease and would accompany each of the doctors on trips.

Dr. Robertson made sure the standards of care provided at the small Fayette hospital were equal to the American College of Surgeons standards, whose accreditation he sought because it was the only accrediting agency for health care facilities at that time. However, the American College of Surgeons would not accredit any hospital smaller than 25 beds. Dr. Robertson, with all his efforts, could not convince them to come to Fayette to survey the McNease-Robertson Hospital. Finally one day, Dr. Jim Mason, a friend and mentor of Dr. Robertson's during his residency program, called Dr. Robertson from Jasper to tell him there was a survey team from the American College of Surgeons conducting a survey at the Jasper hospital. Dr. Robertson immediately went to Jasper and carried patient medical records with him to demonstrate to the surveyors the quality of work being done at his small hospital in Fayette. He was able to persuade the survey team to come to Fayette to conduct the required survey. Meanwhile, a few hectic hours were spent rounding up enough cribs to meet the required number of 25 beds. While conducting its review, the survey team was favorably impressed with everything it saw, especially the completeness of the medical records. The McNease-Robertson Hospital won the distinction of being the smallest hospital in the United States ever accredited by the American College of Surgeons.

Though Dr. Robertson worked very hard to achieve accreditation by the American College of Surgeons, he gave Dr. McNease all the credit for the high standards of care provided at the McNease-Robertson Clinic-Hospital. The two doctors were an excellent health care team.

Dr. Robertson was also active on the state level. He was chairman of the Alabama Hospital Association in

1941-42 and was actively involved in organizing Blue Shield of Alabama.

Dr. Robertson continued his exceptional work for ten years until he was forced to retire in 1947 due to his health. In his ten short years of practice, Dr. Robertson made a profound impact on the medical history of Fayette County. Even in retirement, Dr. Robertson retained his passion for doing what he could in the community. He became the Fayette County Health Officer and in that role placed great emphasis on disease prevention. He took an active interest in politics, which included serving two terms as chairman of the Fayette County Board of Education. He helped organize the Fayette Park and Recreation Board in 1955 and served as its first chairman. He was also interested in civic work and was active in the First United Methodist Church, where he was a board member, trustee, and chairman of the Pastor Parish Relations Committee. Dr. Robertson was noted as an outstanding leader in the community and in 1955 he was chosen by the Exchange Club as the "Man of the Year" for Fayette County.

Dr. John Banks Robertson, Sr. was a determined, passionate individual who sought excellence in everything he did. He loved his family and was a willing and constant supporter in all areas of community.

Henry Gunter Hodo, Jr., MD

General Surgery and Family Practice

Dr. Hodo was born and raised in Millport, Alabama, in Lamar County about 15 miles from Fayette. He graduated from Millport High School in 1932. He attended The University of Alabama and completed his under-graduate degree in 1936. Since this was before the University had a four-year medical school, he remained at the University for the pre-clinical years of medical school and went to the University of Pennsylvania

Henry G. Hodo, Jr., MD

for the clinical years. He returned to Birmingham, Alabama, to the well-known Hillman Hospital for his intern year and three years as a surgery resident.

Dr. Hodo was recognized as an excellent surgeon, even in his residency. Local surgeons practicing in Birmingham came to Hillman just to watch Dr. Hodo perform surgery. After residency, Dr. Hodo served as a surgeon with the Army Medical Corps for two years during World War II, seeing duty in both the European and Pacific Theatres. He was being transferred from Brooke Army General Hospital in San Antonio, Texas, to Fort McPherson, Georgia, when he stopped in Fayette to visit his wife Naomi's relatives at about the time Dr. Banks Robertson retired due to health reasons. While in Fayette, Dr. McNease asked him to do an emergency caesarian section on one of his patients. Dr. McNease saw what a good surgeon Dr. Hodo was and immediately began recruiting him. Within a few months, Dr. Hodo was back in Fayette with his wife Naomi and he was immediately busy with a meaningful practice that would continue for fifty years. "I went to work the day we arrived," Dr. Hodo said. "We stayed in the Brock home (his wife's parents) because there was no place for us to live, but we soon got an apartment," he added.

Dr. Hodo started his practice in Fayette in 1946 and immediately assumed the responsibility of administrator of the McNease-Robertson Hospital in addition to the duties of surgeon. He became one of the community's leading figures.

Dr. Hodo maintained a heavy surgery load, as had Dr. Robertson before him, and also carried out the duties of a family doctor. His typical day started with push-ups and sit-ups before he left home at 5:30 a.m. to make two or three house calls. He usually arrived at the hospital at 7:30 a.m. to perform surgeries before trying to get to his office by noon to see patients. He normally left the office around 7:00 p.m., returned to the hospital for evening rounds, then made four or five more house calls before arriving home for dinner around 10:00 p.m.

Due to Dr. Hodo's long days, he made it clear that

he required fidelity to his routine to stay on schedule. After Fayette County Hospital opened, all doctors were assigned private parking spaces. Dr. Hodo's was near the Emergency Department, and on one occasion Dr. Hodo arrived to find that a visitor had parked in his space. Dr. Hodo pulled his car against the visitor's bumper and proceeded into surgery for half a day.

Dr. Hodo said that in those days the family doctor was not only the healer of sickness, but also a confidante, trusted friend, sounding board, and problem solver for many things not related to a person's physical well-being. "I remember when the old hospital first began charging an emergency room fee," he said, "I was accosted by an irate little lady who thoroughly raked me over the coals because she was charged two dollars, as she said, 'for just settin in the settin room'."

Dr. Hodo became a leading force in developing the new hospital, seeing it arrive as one of the most modern of its day. Dr. Hodo did 500 to 600 surgeries per year and said that his biggest operation was removing a 55-pound fibroid tumor from a woman's abdomen. During his career as a surgeon and family doctor, he performed over 22,000 surgeries and delivered thousands of babies. "Yes, it was exhausting, but you did it because you loved it and because of the gratification you received from it," he said. "You didn't have to worry about government regulations or malpractice. You worried only about the patient and practiced medicine to the very best of your ability."

Dr. Hodo continued the untiring efforts of Dr. McNease and Dr. Robertson to build an excellent health care system in Fayette. His contributions were significant and appreciated. Dr. Hodo was so respected and honored by his peers that, when the doctors occupied a new clinic across from Fayette County Hospital in 1979, they named it the McNease-Hodo Clinic.

As the only surgeon in Fayette for most of his career, Dr. Hodo had a very busy practice, but he was active also in the affairs of professional societies at the local, state, and federal levels. This service included

- President of Fayette County Hospital Medical Staff, where he chaired every medical staff committee and related hospital committees.
- President of the Alabama College of Surgeons.
- Fayette County Hospital Board of Directors from 1976-1984.
- Member of the Southern Medical Association.
- Fellow of both the Southeastern College of Surgeons and the American College of Surgeons.
- Blue Cross/Blue Shield Board of Directors for many years, starting in 1970.
- Recipient of the Ira L. Myers Service Award in 2001 from the Alabama Public Health Association.
- Board of Medical Examiners and State Board of Health, 1970-1991.

Dr. Hodo was twice asked to accept the position of president of the Medical Association of the State of Alabama (MASA), but declined both times, stating he was the only surgeon in Fayette and he could not be away for that length of time.

Dr. Hodo was an active, contributing member of the community all the time he was in Fayette. He and Naomi had one son and two granddaughters, the oldest of which was chosen as a Rhodes Scholar. He was also chairman of the Board of Trustees for the First United Methodist Church in Fayette, a member of the Fayette Area Chamber of Commerce Board of Trustees and Fayette Industrial Development Board, and a charter member of the Fayette Exchange Club. Dr. Hodo retired as a surgeon in December 1983, but continued to see patients in his clinic for another year and assumed the duties of medical director of long term care. His medical career spanned over 50 years.

Soon after Dr. Hodo's retirement and while he was medical director of long term care in 1988, Hospital Administrator John Lucas provided the following tribute to Dr. Hodo in special recognition for his many years of dedication and support:

> *"We are privileged to live in a country that has the finest medical facilities in the world. Fayette County Hospital boasts the latest technological equipment and is the most modern and up-to-date rural institution in the state. We are truly blessed. Such dramatic progress doesn't happen without the courageous and dynamic leadership of individuals who have persevered in developing*

our health care system. We have been so busy
building on the blocks they put in place that
we never have given the recognition they so
richly deserve. I would like to pay tribute to
one of those great pioneers of Fayette County
who has made possible all that we are lucky
enough to take for granted today." In Special
recognition of Dr. Hodo, John Lucas, 1988

When asked about Dr. Hodo, Mrs. Hodo said, "There
are two things about Henry: he works hard and he is
just an all-around good guy." Also, she said, "He worked
hard and should be remembered for all he gave to the
people of this community and should receive all their
appreciation."

In 1997, Dr. Hodo was recognized and honored for
his faithful service of 50 years and the newly constructed
surgery wing at Fayette Medical Center was named after
him. A plaque so designating was placed in the hallway
entering the surgery department with wording as follows:

The Surgical Wing of Fayette Medical Center
is Dedicated to
Henry Gunter Hodo Jr., MD

Who has faithfully served the medical
profession in Fayette County for more than
fifty years and has led a life of the highest
professional and personal merit. Dr. Hodo
is known far and wide for his expertise as

a surgeon and a family physician. He has devoted his adult life to improving the quality of medical care for the people throughout Alabama and has been as pillar of strength and inspiration for other physicians who followed in his footsteps. Much of the success of Fayette Medical Center today can be directly attributed to his strong leadership and involvement. Dedicated June 19, 1997

Dr. Hodo was a man of determination, strong will, and character. He could be a good friend and he enjoyed a little humor along the way, but he also believed that everyone should play by the rules.

Inez Fowler, MD

General Practice, Psychiatry

Dr. Inez Fowler was a native of Fayette County and came from a small family. She never married and had only one sister, but was very self-sufficient. In her years of retirement, she often proclaimed, "I was married to my profession." She had great passionof for her work and gave much of her life to medicine and the people of Fayette County.

Inez Fowler, MD

Dr. Fowler served the Fayette community in three different health care roles. First, she was a laboratory technician at the McNease–Robertson Clinic-Hospital. Later, she became a primary care physician. She finished her medical career as a psychiatrist in private practice.

Dr. Fowler attended The University of Alabama at Tuscaloosa and received her undergraduate degree in 1941. She was accepted to the Medical College of Alabama, but due to the United States' preparations for World War II, which were heightened by the attack on Pearl

Harbor in 1941, the United States Army and Navy took control of medical education and excluded females. This was in keeping with policies to train and draft medical personnel for deployment in war zones, which at the time excluded women. (See William S. Mullins, ed. *Medical Department, United States Army Medical Training in World War II*. Accessed at <u>http://history.amedd.army.</u> <u>mil/booksdocs/wwii/medtrain/ch1.htm</u>.) Instead of going to medical school, Dr. Fowler received training as a laboratory technician. She returned to Fayette and worked in the laboratory of McNease-Robertson Clinic-Hospital until World War II ended in 1945.

When females were again accepted into medical schools in 1945, Dr. Fowler was admitted and had the honor of being the only person from Fayette County to receive a four-year medical scholarship from a government entity, presumably the state of Alabama. That same year, the University of Alabama School of Medicine was relocated from Tuscaloosa to Birmingham and expanded to a full four-year program of study. Dr. Fowler graduated with honors in 1949 among the first class to graduate from this "new" four-year Medical College of Alabama. She stayed in Birmingham and completed an internship at Jefferson-Hillman Hospital where she first met Dr. Richard Rutland, another intern.

The internship was a very strenuous year, especially the obstetrics rotation, with both Dr. Fowler and Rutland carrying heavy workloads. There were only ten interns, a staff half the size needed for a hospital as large as the Jefferson-Hillman Hospital. Two of the interns had been classmates of Dr. Rutland at Tulane, but there was little time to socialize. It was a tough year for both Dr. Fowler and Dr. Rutland.

Following the intern year, Dr. Fowler served as Medical Director/Administrator at the Mobile Red Cross Blood Center for a year before returning to Fayette. "I returned to Fayette to fulfill my life-long dream of practicing medicine with my idol, Dr. Benjamin Wilberne McNease," she said. Dr. Fowler had known Dr. McNease all her life. She had been his patient, had observed and admired his work, and was highly influenced by him in her plans to become a physician.

While in Fayette, Dr. Fowler delivered a large number of babies and said she experienced discrimination for being a female only once when she was called to deliver a baby for a physician who was out of town. The woman's husband ranted and raved, saying that no woman would deliver a baby of his. Dr. Fowler said that she told him that he was free to take his wife elsewhere. The husband grumbled, but allowed her to proceed. Dr. Fowler delivered the child and subsequently delivered two more children for the couple. In those busy early years of practice she did not miss the opportunity to recruit additional help when her colleague from the internship days, Richard Rutland, called to explore the potential for a practice site in Fayette.

In 1958, after six years of practice in Fayette, Dr. Fowler required surgery for a bone tumor. The remaining physicians took on her patient load, and Dr. Breitling was added to the local medical staff in 1959. As much as she loved providing primary care in Fayette with Dr. McNease, Dr. Hodo, and Dr. Rutland, Dr. Fowler discovered her greatest interest was in behavioral medicine. As she recovered from surgery, she applied for and received a scholarship for five years of training in adult and child psychiatry at the University of Alabama School of Medicine in Birmingham. Upon completing training in psychiatry, she directed a mental health service for University of Alabama students in Birmingham for two years. She then established a private practice of psychiatry in Tuscaloosa. At one time, Dr. Fowler was the only person certified in both child and adult psychiatry in Alabama.

Dr. Fowler closed her psychiatric practice in Tuscaloosa and moved back home to Fayette in 1973 to support her father during an illness he contracted and to assume primary family responsibilities related to a niece, with child, who had been abandoned by her husband. While in Fayette, she accepted a part-time position with Northwest Alabama Mental Health Center in Hamilton for one year and also maintained a part-time private psychiatry practice in Fayette. She opened an office in a house across the street from her home. She was appreciated for her expertise in psychiatry, but had to reduce her work load in her later years.

"I lived the life of a woman who dared to enter the male-dominated field of medicine and to work harder to achieve," Dr. Fowler said at the end of her career. She also made the observation that "many more women have entered medicine and have been accepted, for the most part, as equals, though still having to prove themselves capable."

Dr. Fowler was a person of exceptional knowledge and ability. She was a very independent lady with strong fortitude and she cared deeply for her profession, her patients, and family. She was loyal to the Fayette Church of Christ.

Richard Oliver Rutland, Jr., MD

Family Practice

Dr. Richard Oliver Rutland, Jr. was born in the small town of Eufaula in Southeast Alabama, in 1926—the same year that Dr. McNease came to Fayette. "I hero worshiped Paul P. Salter, my family doctor in Eufaula," Dr. Rutland said. Dr. Salter was a family doctor and surgeon, a typical generalist of his day, and the father and grandfather of surgeons. He greatly influenced Dr.

Richard O. Rutland, Jr., MD

Rutland's decision to go into medicine and also to go to medical school at Tulane University, Dr. Salter's alma mater. "Dr. Salter set my course on entering a general practice of medicine," Dr. Rutland said. "He was the type of doctor you grew up with and the kind of doctor you wanted to be."

Dr. Rutland did not complete high school due to the certainty that he would be drafted into the armed forces during World War II as soon as he was old enough. He knew he wanted to be a doctor and he was instructed to complete as much of his education as possible before being drafted. Needing fifteen high school credits to be admitted to college, he worked diligently and went to summer school at Tuscaloosa High School for two classes to complete those requirements. One of the classes at Tuscaloosa High was an English class where he met Nancy Babb, the beautiful young lady from Texas who later would become a large part of his life.

Dr. Rutland passed the college entrance exams easily and attended The University of Alabama for just over one year before joining the V-12 Navy College Training Program. This program was designed to augment the flow of college-educated commissioned officers needed by the Navy by supporting young enlisted men to attend college. (Alison C. V-12: The Navy College Training Program, http://homepages.rootsweb.ancestry. com/~uscnrotc/V-12/v12-his.htm). He was not deployed immediately in the war, because the Navy wanted him to be a doctor. Instead, they sent him to Duke University where he completed the premedical education requirements needed to enter medical school. He received active duty pay while in the V-12 program, which helped greatly with college expenses. Unlike high school and college, there were no shortcuts to the four years of medical education at Tulane, where the Navy sent him. However, World War II ended in 1945, his freshman year in medical school, and he was taken off active duty, which meant no more military pay. Fortunately, his parents could help with his medical school expenses.

During the first two years of pre-clinical medical training, he received a good foundation in the sciences, especially pharmacology. However, the patient contact of the two clinical years made those his favorite years of medical school. He enjoyed most the summers during these clinical years when he returned home to work with his childhood hero and mentor, Dr. Paul Salter.

Dr. Rutland received the Doctor of Medicine degree from Tulane School of Medicine in 1949. In the late 1940s, Tulane was considered possibly the best medical school in the South. Dr. Rutland said of his time at Tulane, "I was fortunate to have learned from some of the finest medical minds in the world." One was Dr. Alton Ochsner, the famous surgeon for whom the renowned Ochsner Clinic is named. Ochsner contributed to discovering the connection between smoking and lung cancer.

Dr. Rutland also spoke of his classmates, saying, "My classmates were exceedingly bright, fascinating people." His most interesting classmate was Dr. Robert W. Brown, better known as Bobby Brown, the third baseman for the New York Yankees with a batting average of .500 in the World Series. Bobby's teammates included Mickey Mantle, Joe DiMaggio, Phil Rizzuto, Whitey Ford, and Yogi Berra. Bobby alternated playing baseball for six months with attending Tulane for six months, until he completed his medical degree.

From Tulane, Dr. Rutland came to Birmingham to the Jefferson-Hillman Hospital for his internship. There he met Dr. Inez Fowler and they became close friends. The internship program was seriously understaffed, so they came to rely on each other to survive the workload. It was a trying year.

Dr. Rutland has enjoyed telling about a remarkable event that occurred during his intern year, during a very busy obstetrics rotation. As he walked past an open window, a loud racket from the parking lot caught his attention. He looked out to see a winsome young woman scratching off in a sporty red car. He quickly identified her as Nancy Babb, his attractive classmate in English at Tuscaloosa High School. It did not take long for them to renew their acquaintance and become close friends.

The Korean War started in 1950 during his intern year, and Dr. Rutland was placed back on active duty. The benefits of active duty, even while still an intern, made it feasible for him to consider marriage. Nancy agreed, and they were soon wed. At the end of the internship, he was required to serve two years in support of the Navy. His first duty assignment was Key West, Florida, which offered the young couple the honeymoon trip they never had. From Key West, Dr. Rutland was scheduled to receive orders to ship out. But when he realized he would miss the birth of their first child, he requested and received a change of orders that delayed his departure. Later, he served in both the Pacific and Korean Theaters. During one excursion when he was the only Medical Officer aboard an amphibious cargo ship, it became necessary for him to remove the hot appendix of a Navy chief petty officer. It was a trying experience. The operating room conditions were very poor and the ship was rocking. Dr. Rutland had only his internship year behind him, but he had assisted surgeons at Jefferson-Hillman Hospital. With five corpsmen to assist him, only one of whom had ever helped in surgery, he braved the stressful task and got a good outcome.

After the Navy, Dr. Rutland determined to complete two years of general practice residency. The first year was at Bakersfield, California, and the second was at the University of Colorado in Denver. He and Nancy were not happy with Bakersfield-- it rained only once while they were there, but they experienced frightening earthquakes and aftershocks. The only thing good to come out of Bakersfield for them was a second child, a daughter. They liked Denver much better.

After residency, Dr. Rutland intended to follow the model of Dr. Salter and complete additional training in surgery. He began a discussion with Dr. Champ Lyons, Chairman of the Department of Surgery at Jefferson-Hillman Hospital. While still in the discussion over three (Dr. Lyons' preference) versus two years (Dr. Rutland's intention) of surgery training, Dr. Rutland met Dr. John Hodo. Dr. John Hodo told Dr. Rutland about his brother, Henry, a general surgeon in Fayette, and how he would be an excellent surgeon with whom to train. He also said that Fayette needed a doctor just like Dr. Rutland. Dr. Rutland called Dr. Inez Fowler, his friend and workmate from their internship who was then in Fayette, and asked if there was an opportunity in Fayette. Her response was, "How fast can you get here?"

It was 1954; Dr. Rutland did not know that he was beginning a lifetime of work in Fayette, Alabama, or that he was so well prepared for the task. Like those before him, he had dedicated his life to the medical profession, but he thought that he coming to Fayette was to learn surgery skills from Dr. Hodo and fulfill his dream of becoming like Dr. Salter.

Dr. Rutland and Dr. B.W. McNease

He thought he would be moving on to another small town to practice. However, while learning from Dr. Hodo and providing family care, his own family continued to grow. He and Nancy added another daughter and son in short order. (Dr. Rutland delivered his son because the baby boy was early and Nancy's doctor was out of town at an Alabama-Auburn football game.) Along the way, his ambitions changed, Fayette grew to fulfill the dream he had pursued since childhood, and Alabama was to witness the growth of an icon in family medicine.

Dr. Rutland assisted Dr. Hodo on numerous cases and performed many surgeries himself, finding contentment in his work and in the community. He once said "My infatuation with becoming a physician was predicated on learning to relate to people. I gradually learned to walk figuratively in the shoes of my patients, whatever their status in life, and yet maintain a reasonable degree of objectivity." And his own influence began to be felt in the community as he had felt that of Dr. Salter. For example, while still in his early years of practice in Fayette, Dr. Rutland made a house call in Kennedy, Alabama, at the home of an elderly gentleman. The man's grandson was there and observed Dr. Rutland as he cared for his grandfather. When Dr. Rutland left, the young boy determined, "I want to be a doctor like that man." The grandson, William A. Curry, was to create his own professional identity including 15 years of practice in Carrollton, Alabama, leadership in the Medical Association of the State of Alabama, the deanship of the University of Alabama College of Community Health Sciences, and higher administration at the UAB School of Medicine.

Dr. Rutland's career encompassed the great change in medicine that occurred following World War II. When he began practice at the McNease-Hodo Clinic, he did his own x-rays, developed them, and read them himself. At the time of his retirement, he could order a CT or MRI scan at the hospital and expect a timely interpretation of the results provided by a board certified radiologist located miles away in another city via telemedicine.

As he mastered his art in rural family practice, Dr. Rutland's influence expanded through the community and the medical profession. Because of their confidence in him, his peers propelled him to leadership in the state's family physicians' organization. In 1961, he was elected president of the Alabama Chapter of the American Academy of Family Physicians. While serving in this capacity, he became concerned about the growing trend among newly educated physicians to sub-specialize, instead of pursuing general practice. His childhood role model and his experience caring for the residents of Fayette confirmed for him that physicians who were broadly trained to care for the large majority of health care concerns experienced by most patients was the principal medical education need in the state. He expressed this view broadly and looked for the opportunity to lead Alabama's medical education program in this direction. When fourth-year medical student Lee Taylor in Birmingham started the push for a clinical rotation in an outlying area, Dr. Rutland was quick to respond. In 1966, he worked with the University of Alabama School of Medicine, located in Birmingham, to have Fayette approved as a preceptor site for fourth-year medical students. In the fifteen years that followed, almost fifty students and family practice residents took clinical rotations in Fayette, learning from accomplished local physicians in their offices, the hospital, and community settings. The people of Fayette were proud partners in the effort to produce physicians who understood the lives of rural Alabamians and were prepared to serve them.

When need for family doctors for rural areas became an issue in Alabama in the late 1960s, Dr. Rutland was an acknowledged leader in this field. Soon he was enlisted by The University of Alabama in the effort to establish a new medical education program for that purpose. In 1969, UA President David Mathews involved him and Dr. John Burnum, a Tuscaloosa Internist, in planning and recruiting a dean to establish the College of Community Health Sciences (CCHS) and Tuscaloosa Family Practice Residency at The University of Alabama. Dr. William R. Willard, who had recently retired as the dean of the University of Kentucky School of Medicine, was selected as founding dean of CCHS in 1971. Dr. Willard is credited for making the medical education program for students in their clinical years and the Family Medicine residency in Tuscaloosa a reality.

The academic specialty of Family Medicine was still very new at the time and there were few seasoned role models within medical school ranks. Dr. Willard convinced Dr. Rutland in 1972 to give up two days per week from his practice in Fayette to teach family practice residents. He served as the director of the Tuscaloosa Family Practice Residency from 1973-75. On the days that he was in Tuscaloosa, colleagues in Fayette, especially doctors Breitling and Hodo, provided coverage for his patients.

Dr. Rutland is widely recognized for his central role in getting CCHS off to a good start. In the history of the college, titled *A Special Kind of Doctor*, he is pictured prominently with other college fathers including President Mathews, Dr. John Burnum, and Dr. Bill Owings. It was extra work to help build a medical education program for family doctors, but he was also to gain from this labor.

Dr. Michael McBrearty, the first doctor to complete the residency program in Tuscaloosa, was deeply affected by Dr. Rutland's leadership and, during his last year in residency, married Dr. Rutland's oldest daughter, Cindy.

The couple provided Dr. and Mrs. Rutland with four grandchildren, including one who attended medical school at CCHS and took Family Medicine training in Colorado, following his grandfather's footsteps. Dr. Rutland has been privileged to see family doctors populating many of Alabama's rural communities as an outgrowth of his seminal work. Three of these board certified family physicians have taken residence to practice and raise families in Fayette--Dr. Garry Magouirk, Dr. Fred Yerby, and Dr. Greg Stidham.

Dr. Rutland with *A Special Kind of Doctor*

Resuming his fulltime practice, Dr. Rutland was recognized as the model of a true family doctor. He provided health care services to his patients from cradle to grave. In the later years of his practice, he transitioned into long term care practice focusing on nursing home patients. During that time he was a facilitator, motivator, defender, and outstanding champion for long term care. Under his guidance, the Fayette Nursing Home consistently received excellent ratings from the State Department of Public Health and the Joint Commission on Accreditation of Health Care Facilities. The nursing staff, medical staff, and administration greatly appreciated his consistent leadership. Dr. Rutland retired in August 2008 after 54 years of dedicated service. But even in retirement, he has remained active by keeping up with current events, being an active member of the Fayette Area Chamber of Commerce, consulting with CCHS, and staying involved with the community and his church.

Dr. Rutland and Nancy have played an important role in the community, their church, and in local school affairs. In 1960, they were voted "Man and Woman of the Year." In 2012, they were inducted into the Fayette County Athletic Hall of Fame because Mrs. Rutland had done so much work teaching swimming lessons at the city pool and the Bevill State Community College. Dr. Rutland had coached a diving team and had worked with the Fayette and Hubbertville football teams as the team doctor and in developing new team policies regarding athletic physicals. Dr. Rutland was a trustee at the Fayette County High School for several years. He was active also in the First United Methodist Church and held several positions there. He is best known, however, for his compassionate care of his patients and being a loving family community doctor.

Dr. Rutland won the affection of his community and the state as one of their beloved family physicians. He has been recognized widely for his exemplary service in this role. In 1981, he was named the Alabama Family Doctor of the Year and was chosen by *Good Housekeeping* and the American Academy of Family Physicians as the 1981 Family Doctor of the Year. The latter award was presented to him in the office of Dr. Edward N. Brandt, Assistant Secretary for Health of the United States Department of Health and Human Services in Washington, DC on August 7, 1981. Other recognition included

- The Rural Health Provider Exceptional Achievement Award in 2003, from the Alabama Rural Health Association.
- The Rural Medical Scholars Program Sage Award in 2005, from the University of Alabama Rural Medical Scholars Program for contributions to the development of rural medical education in Alabama.
- The Paul W. Burleson Award in 2006, from the Medical Association of the State of Alabama "in recognition of a medical career that encompasses not only high ethical and professional standards in patient care, but includes extraordinary service to physician organizations at the county, state and national levels."

A man of courage and conviction, Richard O. Rutland, Jr., MD, is widely loved and respected and has contributed to the betterment of health care for people in Fayette, Alabama, and the country.

Harold E. Breitling, MD

General Practice

Dr. Harold E. Breitling was born and raised in Demopolis, Alabama. He was affected by asthma in his formative years. Dr. William Cocke delivered Dr. Breitling and was

his family doctor. Dr. Cocke visited the Breitling home numerous times early in the morning hours when Dr. Breitling was having difficulty breathing as a child. However, asthma did not keep him from being active in sports. He played high school football, but preferred baseball because it did not affect his asthma as much. His love of sports

Harold E. Breitling MD

became even more evident during his medical career.

Dr. Cocke was one of three physicians who had a great influence on Dr. Breitling's decisions concerning a career in medicine. Dr. Breitling wanted to be a doctor and help people like Dr. Cocke had helped him. "But I never thought it would be possible," Dr. Breitling said.

Dr. Breitling sometimes saw Dr. Arlington Henry Bobo, Sr., because of his asthma. Dr. Bobo also was influential in Dr. Breitling's decision to become a doctor. Dr. Bobo made a lasting impression on Dr. Breitling by prescribing an inhalation spray that helped control his symptoms. (Later, when he was in practice, Dr. Breitling said he often thought about Dr. Bobo prescribing the asthma spray for him when he prescribed the same asthma spray for his own patients.) Dr. Breitling also became a close friend with A. H. "Bill" Bobo, Jr., Dr. Bobo's son.

Dr. Bobo was originally from Covin, Alabama in Fayette County. He received his Doctor of Medicine degree from the Birmingham Medical School, which existed from 1894 to 1915 and closed during the era of reform in medical education fueled by the Flexner Report. Dr. Bobo began to practice medicine in Jefferson County in 1911. Later, he moved to Demopolis, Alabama, where he had a successful practice for 20 years and was active in the community. He was named the Demopolis "Man of the Year" in 1948, but due to poor health retired and returned to Covin in Fayette County. He was active in the Covin Baptist Church and was a deacon there. He passed away at the McNease-Robertson Hospital as the result of a heart attack in 1953.

Dr Julian Howell, who practiced at Baptist Hospital in Selma, was another doctor who influenced Dr. Breitling. Dr. Howell was a pioneer in having medical students do rotations away from the medical school with community doctors as part of their training. Dr. Breitling, the second student that Dr. Howell precepted, worked with Dr. Howell the summer between his junior and senior years in medical school. Dr. Howell allowed Dr. Breitling, the medical student, to observe him seeing patients and to scrub in on surgery cases during that very educational summer.

Dr. Breitling started his formal education at Livingston University, which he attended for two years. He then attended The University of Alabama for two years and received a bachelor's degree in Chemistry. He then went to the University of Alabama School of Medicine and Hillman Clinics, which later became central components of the University of Alabama at Birmingham or UAB, for his four years of medical school. In 1957, he received the Doctor of Medicine degree. Dr. Breitling went to Caraway Methodist Medical Center for his intern year in 1957-58 and in 1958-59 he stayed on at Caraway for a residency year in internal medicine.

In the fall of 1956, he was attracted to Pat Newton, a nursing student. Their relationship grew over the next year and on December 1, 1957, they were married. The couple eventually had three children.

Pat's mother, Dr. Breitling's mother-in-law who lived in Fayette, suggested that he call Dr. McNease about a possible practice opportunity. After talking to Dr. McNease, the first person he met when he arrived in Fayette was Bill "Swamp" Sanders, an independent insurance agent, who convinced him what a great community Fayette was. Dr. Breitling and Pat moved to Fayette where their family soon became comfortable.

Dr. Breitling said "he most enjoyed practicing medicine like he did when he first started, when the only thing he had to concern himself with was the patient." He showed little interest in affairs of the organized profession, although he did maintain a membership in the Medical Association of the State of Alabama, the American Medical Association, and the Alabama Association of Family Practice. Though he disliked going to meetings, he knew someone needed to represent the interest of doctors like those in Fayette at the state and national levels. His partners took on this responsibility, and so it was a perfect match.

Dr. Breitling practiced for 20 years in the old McNease-Hodo Clinic and spent another 32 years in the Clinic at its new location at 1716 Temple Avenue North. He also had privileges at Fayette County Hospital. When Dr. Breitling first started his practice in the McNease Clinic he saw only ten to twelve patients per day. This low patient census was primarily due to the fact that he was sharing practice with his medical school classmate, Dr. John Davis, who had joined the clinic just two month before him. When Dr. Davis went back to medical school to train as an ear, nose, and throat specialist, Dr. Breitling soon had a very busy practice.

Dr. Breitling said many of his patients came from outside the city of Fayette and from surrounding counties. Many were athletes from Berry and Hubbertville high schools. Dr. Breitling made a considerable number of house calls during his long career, reminiscent of his own childhood mentor who visited his home many times when he had asthma.

Dr. Breitling's greatest pleasure was in sports medicine. He dedicated himself for the first 30 years of his practice to attending almost all Fayette County High School basketball and football games. He was inducted into the Fayette County Athletic Hall of Fame for his dedication to and support of Fayette County sports.

Dr. Breitling often made house calls.

In addition to his practice, Dr. Breitling was a successful businessman and forestry farmer. He was an advocate for preserving the beauty of Fayette County's natural landscape.

Dr. Breitling had a remarkable 52-year career in Fayette. During that period, he spent more time at work than he did at home. He said Pat was mother and father to their children while he was doing what the practice demanded. Dr. Breitling is warmly remembered by the community. He made many friends. In retirement, he found time and opportunity for visiting, something he had little time for during his very busy career. And he could give more time to his hobby as a Civil War enthusiast. His grandchildren also became top priority. He was quick to honor the contributions of all the employees at the McNease Clinic, the McNease-Hodo Clinic, and the Fayette County Hospital. He also expressed his love and great appreciation for Pat's selfless devotion to minding everything at home while he was at the hospital.

Jon Emory Sanford, MD

Family Practice

Jon Emory Sanford, MD was born and raised in Walker County, Alabama. His father was a school principal, a math teacher, and a minister. His family lived on a farm eight miles north of Jasper where he learned the value of hard work. Dr. Sanford attended Walker County High School where he was an excellent student, student body president, and a football player. He was captain of the defense-minded team that allowed only two touchdowns on the way to the state championship among Alabama's larger schools.

Dr. Sanford was impressed by Coach Paul "Bear" Bryant who, on his first trip to Alabama from Texas A&M, made a speech at the Walker County High School Vikings' football banquet and presented the State Champ-ionship trophy. It was not a coincidence that Coach Bryant's trip also included the recruitment of Jon's long-time friend, Bill Richardson. Bill was named Mr. Football-State of Alabama in

Jon Emory Sanford, M.D.

1958 and later played on Coach Bryant's first national championship team of 1961. Dr. Sanford told his dad after hearing Coach Bryant speak that he wanted to walk on at Alabama the following year. The next day, he was called to the principal's office where the principal told him that he was too little to play SEC ball. His coach said, "You're too slow," and his dad said, "You're not going." Subsequently, Dr. Sanford accepted an offer of a football scholarship to Samford University. However, just as fall practice was set to begin, the school canceled all sport scholarships due to hardships associated with the campus' move from East Lake to Homewood. However, Dr. Sanford received a call from Dr. Evan Zeiger, Sr., vice-president for financial affairs and athletic director, who was heavily involved in the move and who said Dr. Sanford could receive one of Samford's academic scholarships. Along with the scholarship, he was given a job at the local hospital that provided him with room and board and a salary of $100 per month. Dr. Zeiger became a life-long friend and mentor. Dr. Sanford said Dr. Zeiger was very instrumental in him going to medical school. (Dr. Zeiger's own son would become a noted neurosurgeon in Birmingham, and die tragically with his wife in the crash of his single-engine propeller airplane.)

While at Samford, Jon met Mary Anne Thomas, a pharmacy student from Birmingham. He was her lab instructor in Chemistry. In 1960, they married and subsequently became proud parents of three children and grandparents of nine grandchildren.

Receiving the Bachelor of Science in Chemistry in

1962, Dr. Sanford went to the University of Alabama School of Medicine and received his Doctor of Medicine in 1966. He completed an internship from 1966-67 at University Hospital, Birmingham, Alabama. He, along with other medical students, was inducted into the Army Reserves to await active duty upon completion of their internships. However, his activation was deferred, thus Dr. Sanford opened a general practice in Gordo, Alabama, in neighboring Pickens County, where he stayed for five years.

During a family practice meeting in Orlando, Florida, Dr. Sanford approached Dr. Richard Rutland with the idea of moving his practice to Fayette. Dr. Sanford and his family moved to Fayette in 1972 where he developed and has maintained a busy practice. Now, after 47 years of practice, Dr. Sanford is beginning to scale back.

Dr. Sanford's practice was typical. He had a busy clinic and hospital practice. During the twenty-one years that he maintained an obstetrical practice, he delivered approximately 2500 babies, over 200 the final year. He also has maintained a large nursing home patient load.

During his career, Dr. Sanford has been generous with his time, support, and leadership to maintain quality services in Fayette. He supported and defended the nursing home when onerous and impractical regulations threatened the quality and service that Fayette County Nursing Home residents and families appreciated. When the hospital was considering the purchase of its first CT scanner, he flew his private plane, at his own expense, with the hospital administrator, radiologist, and surgeon to Chattanooga, Tennessee and on to Athens, Georgia to evaluate the technology and machines available.

Dr. Sanford served in many positions of leadership in the hospital and nursing home. He served on the medical staff as president and member of the executive committee, surgery committee, and others. He was chairman of the quality assurance committee, medical director for Fayette Medical Center Hospice, and chairman of the Fayette Medical Center Board. In the latter position, he worked with administration to implement a master facility plan for construction valued at over $30 million. The plan resulted in a new kitchen, front entrance with lobby, medical records department, new administrative suite, and twenty-one additional nursing home beds.

Dr. Sanford's professional participation and leadership expanded into state and national medical organizations. These included

1973-1996	Member, Alabama Academy of Family Physicians (AAFP)
1974-1977	AAFP Education Committee
1977-1978	AAFP President
1978-1980	AAFP Board of Chairman
1981-1989 g	Board Member, Mutual Assurance Society of Alabama Underwriting Committee, Mutual Assurance Society of Alabama Claims Committee, Mutual Assurance Society of Alabama
1983-1989	Alternate delegate to the American Medical Association (AMA)

1989-1999	Delegate to AMA
1996	Chair, Reference Committee F of the AMA, representative from Medical Association of the State of Alabama (MASA) for 12 years on Reference Committee A (socio-economic affairs) of the AMA
1989-1996	Board of Censors, Medical Association of Alabama, State Committee of Public Health, Alabama Board of Medical Examiners
1996-2004	Member and chair, Physicians Recovery Network of MASA
2001-2002	President of the Medical Association of the State of Alabama

At the Medical Association of the State of Alabama (MASA) annual meeting in 2001, the House of Delegates and College of Counselors elected Dr. Jon Sanford president of the Medical Association State of Alabama. This is the highest position in organized medicine in Alabama for a physician. This achievement was recognized, and he was honored with a reception at the Fayette Civic Center on July 15, 2001, with his family, colleagues, patients, and friends there to congratulate him.

On June 30, 2001, at his induction into the presidency of MASA, Dr. Sanford made a speech to the association including the following:

[Our profession] is about a relationship, a commitment, a promise that each and every member of this medical profession made when we earned the title "Doctor of Medicine." I suggest to you that the essential ingredient is a sick patient that needs and seeks care by a physician who has pride of professionalism and the spirit of servanthood.

I want to stir in you that pride you felt when you saw that you did indeed possess abilities to make people well and to give comfort and hope where there had only been pain and distress. Which of you does not inhale with pride as you recall your early victories over illness, pain, and death, when you have brought comfort to distraught parents of a sick child, or reassured an aged patient that you would be there when he/she needed you? Because of your training, your skill, and your faithfulness to the contract and promise you made when you took the Hippocratic Oath, you answered that call, fulfilled your duty, and saved a life. Thousands of times we have renewed and sustained that precious contract called "the Physician-Patient relationship" when we sit and listen, make eye contact, communicate expertly, apply hands, order tests and procedures applying the wonders of

*science and technology to our time honored
skills in the art of medicine.*

Dr. Sanford's roles in professional leadership were
time-consuming, requiring the support of his partners
and colleagues to maintain the continuity of his practice.
Though his practice group dissolved in 1990 and in 2001
he relocated from the McNease-Hodo Clinic to 17th
Court NE, his colleagues continued to work cooperatively
with him. Because he was a private pilot and had his own
plane, he minimized the time away from practice with
the trips to Montgomery and other distant professional
meeting locations.

Dr. Sanford proved to be a man of broad intellect and
great compassion. He was accepted as a statesman and
leader. He supported the University of Alabama College
of Community Health Sciences as an adjunct faculty
member and precepted fourth-year medical students,
family practice residents, and nurse practitioner students.
Beyond the bounds of his profession, he gave of himself
to community and church. He became a member of the
Fayette Church of Christ, where he was a deacon for
ten years, before becoming an Elder. His ministerial
role led him to preach, conduct funerals, and serve in
other church activities. A man of faith himself, he once
baptized a patient, who had made a profession of faith and
confession of sin, in the whirlpool at the hospital.

As of this writing, Dr. Sanford's career has included
42 years associated with Fayette Medical Center. He is
known as a man who loves his profession, takes great

pride in carrying out his duties, and has great compassion for his patients. He well deserves the trust of his colleagues and community who have elevated him to positions of authority and who revere him.

Jon Emory Sanford, M.D.

Employees of the McNease-Robertson-Hodo Clinic-Hospital

The McNease-Robertson-Hodo Clinic-Hospital existed as such from 1937 until September 24, 1958, before being replaced by the Fayette County Hospital. At that time, the physicians' offices remained at the clinic and some of the old hospital area also was converted to clinic space. The extremely loyal and dedicated employees of the McNease-Robertson-Hodo Clinic-Hospital worked long, difficult hours. They found value and meaning in their work, saying the work was enjoyable and that they loved their jobs. There was a family atmosphere, a sense of community with shared feelings of concern and affection among themselves and the medical staff for the patients.

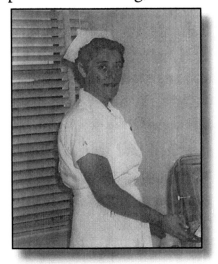

Mrs. Blanche Whitley

A typical day at the McNease-Robertson-Hodo Clinic-Hospital started with Nurse Othelia Whitley's arrival from the nursing quarters, which was a house behind the hospital for all the nurses. Othelia prepared for the day's surgery, which often would go from the early morning to late into the night.

Nurse Lola Allen Collins was the first nurse anesthetist and nursing supervisor. Mrs. Blanche Simpson Whitley later assumed the position of nursing supervisor, serving in that role until the hospital closed. She then moved to Fayette County Hospital and Nursing Home, where she was director of nursing until she retired. Mrs. Whitley insisted on having good nurses. She wanted nurses who would work hard and she screened them closely. While at the clinic-hospital, Mrs. Whitley only employed diploma nurses, with three years formal training in an approved school. The nursing school where most of the nurses trained was in Jasper, Alabama, where Mrs. Whitley had trained also. The diploma nurse was comparable to today's BSN nurse. Their training included the same clinical time as a registered nurse, but not as much classroom time.

Mrs. Whitley was never seen at work when she was not wearing a white nurse's cap and dress uniform, all starched and ironed. She saw the day come when nurses wore pantsuits and took off their caps, but she fought this trend in professional fashion to the end and never agreed that it was correct.

Mrs. Whitley was a tough lady and ruled with an iron fist, but she also had a large heart and great compassion for the patients. She protected patients with the same enthusiasm that she ruled her nurses. Mrs. Whitley was constantly out on the hospital floor observing what was happening and visiting patients. Once, she stepped into a patient's room to find a young boy standing in the corner visiting a patient with his parents. She quickly explained to the boy and his parents, as only she could, that the boy could not be in a patient room until after he was twelve years old. The young boy and his parents tried to explain that he was twelve, but she would not hear it. Mrs. Whitley was a very determined woman, and soon enough, the young gentleman was returned to the lobby.

Maintaining a wholesome and pleasing food service was a very important part of the daily activity at the clinic-hospital from which patients and staff benefitted. There was a large dining table where the doctors and nurses would gather for meals and to discuss care of patients. It was a family dining atmosphere. Dr. McNease, Dr. Robertson, or Dr. Hodo would sit at the head of the table. Jet Kennedy and her sister, Sis Kennedy, prepared delicious meals for the patients, doctors, and other employees, as well as sharing in housekeeping duties.

Wiley Clemons and Lester Bailey helped with housekeeping and maintenance of both the clinic and hospital. They also served as orderlies. Lester, a quick learner, was very helpful to the doctors. Dr. Robertson trained Wiley to do certain procedures and he became the official cast and catheter person. Wiley's wife, Florence, included homemade rolls every day in his lunch. There was a consensus that they were the best rolls in the world, probably because they were cooked with pure lard.

Danylu Nichols and Mildred Dodd, who worked on clinic charges, staffed the business office. Danylu worked closely with all the doctors with their patient accounts. Other business office personnel who worked at different times included Diane Dudley, Hazell White, Mavis Black, Imogene Dudley, Sally Smith, and Jane Edmonds.

Dr. Inez Fowler directed the lab before she went to medical school. Reedus Wheat came on board in 1956, just a few years before the new hospital opened, and made a life-long career for himself in the lab. When Reedus first came to work, he sutured patients when the doctors were in surgery or otherwise busy. The doctors produced and developed x-rays themselves until Reedus took on this responsibility. When he began doing x-rays, the doctors bought Reedus a new x-ray machine. Elese Ehl, Jack Allison, and Francis Maddison were other employees who staffed the lab and x-ray services.

Doctor's offices in the clinic-hospital required nurses and secretaries. Some of these were Dixie Hollingsworth and Nola Morton for Dr. McNease, Charlotte Moore for Dr. Hodo, Doris Wilson and Annie Lee Estes for Dr. Rutland, and Rose Ann Chambless and Louise Collier for Dr. Breitling. Lucille Gentry, Travis Davis, Lowell Neal, Maude Howton, and several more not able to be identified here worked for different doctors at different times. Rocky Brand was a transcriptionist.

Those who worked at the clinic-hospital describe memories of a family-like atmosphere among the professional and employee staffs, a feeling that did not fully transfer to the new hospital. These employees are remembered for the important roles they held, how well they performed them, and their great passion for their work. Theirs were jobs well done in service to their community. Those employees that moved to the new Fayette County Hospital when it opened said that the atmosphere just wasn't the same there.

The New Fayette County Hospital

Fayette County, Alabama, has a long history of outstanding medical professionals who have displayed dedication to their profession, commitment to the community, and compassion for their patients. They have served with passion and exceptional skills, starting with Dr. B. W. McNease, Fayette's "father of modern medicine," and including those who have followed him. They worked long, tiring days in providing health care to the people in the Fayette area.

Dr. Banks Robertson, Sr. joined Dr. McNease, and came to share his vision of improving health care in and around Fayette County. Dr. McNease and Dr. Robertson were responsible for increasing the community's awareness and understanding of quality medical care through the priority and effort they placed on having the 17-bed McNease-Robertson hospital accredited by the American College of Surgeons. This standard of quality of care has been maintained continuously until the present time. From its beginning in 1958, Fayette County Hospital has never failed to be accredited by the Joint Commission of Health Care Organizations, which is the accrediting organization that followed the American College of Surgeons.

In addition, the nursing home has excelled in its licensure, certification, and Life Safety Code surveys conducted by the State Department of Public Health. The hospital and nursing home have consistently demonstrated the highest of quality standards.

The doctors at the McNease clinic worked faithfully in support of the clinic-hospital. They were very proud of being accredited by the American College of Surgeons and having it known that they were providing the highest quality of care. However, at one visit of the accrediting surveyors, the small hospital was warned that it was not completely meeting all the current standards. The disqualification was not because of any failure to meet quality of care standards or not keeping proper medical records. The disqualification came about because the American College of Surgeons had adopted the existing National Fire Protection Association Standards. Fayette hospital's brick veneer over wood construction did not meet the current fire safety standards. The small hospital would have to take corrective action on the deficiencies or it would not continue to be certified. With this notice, the doctors informed the community of the hospital's failure to meet certification requirements and of the need for a new hospital. They immediately began to make the dream of a new hospital become a reality.

At the time, Joseph Lister Hill was Alabama's U.S. senator, who exercised a powerful influence in biomedical research and health care. The Hospital Survey and Construction Act of 1946 was known as the Hill–Burton Act because of his influence. The Act resulted in the provision of federal grants and guaranteed loans to states to improve and build hospitals throughout the nation, hoping to achieve four-and-one-half beds per 1,000 people. The states could allocate the available money to municipalities to build hospitals. Fayette soon learned that federal Hill-Burton funds were available for constructing the planned hospital, but the county would have to provide matching funds for the federal and state funding that would be available.

Without a ready source of such funding, the Fayette county government felt a tax would be necessary to raise the required matching funds. Clyde Cargile, Probate Judge of Fayette County at the time, and the County Commission proposed on October 1, 1954, that a vote be placed before the county to approve a tax to raise the funds needed. The citizens of Fayette County voted to approve, as stated on the ballot

> *a special tax of 4 mils on each dollar of taxable property in Fayette County to be used solely for acquiring by purchase, lease or otherwise, constructing, operating, equipping or maintaining county medical facilities.*

The tax was used to repay the Citizens Bank for a loan that secured matching funds for the Hill-Burton monies. This four mils tax has continued to be a controversy. After the loan was paid, the county continued to receive the tax even after construction of the hospital was complete. Later, the Probate Judge made a request to the Attorney

General to ask if the funds could be used for other health purposes, and the Attorney General said they could. Supporters of the hospital continue to believe these funds should come to the hospital. This issue is still unresolved.

As a requirement of the Hill-Burton Act, when Fayette County Hospital began operation it was necessary to provide care to indigent patients in an amount equal to the Hill-Burton funds secured. When the project was completed, the funds from each source were $358,422 in federal funds, $32,100 from the state, and $178,178 from the county, which included the purchase of the original five-acre site. This total of $568,700 was used to construct the hospital and purchase equipment. The value of the facility has consistently increased from this time, and the Hill-Burton funds have been matched with indigent care.

The Fayette community was very proud to see a new Fayette County Hospital growing up in what had been a cornfield just north of Fayette. It was a substantial modern brick building with a large parking lot. The second floor room on top of the building for mechanical equipment, locally called "the penthouse," made the building look much larger. Actually, it was a small hospital--only one nurse's station and a one-room emergency room. There was one room each for surgery and for obstetrical deliveries. Even the corridors were narrow at only seven feet wide.

A two-foot sprig was set in the front lawn of the new hospital. It would eventually grow into an expansive sugar maple tree bearing beautiful orange leaves each fall. It was an exciting time in 1958 for everyone in the community as they awaited the opening of the new hospital. It started small, but soon began to grow.

On June 9, 1958, the Fayette County Medical Society met at the Fayette County Health Department for an organizational meeting of the Fayette County Hospital medical staff in preparation for the hospital being in operation. Medical Staff officers were elected--Dr. H. G. Hodo, Jr. as president and Dr. Inez Fowler as secretary-treasurer. Other medical staff members present were Dr. B. W. McNease, Dr. R. O. Rutland, Jr., and Dr. J. D. Scrivner. (Dr. Scrivner's practice was located nearby in Berry, Alabama.) Medical staff bylaws, rules, and regulations were adopted at the meeting.

Fayette County Hospital- 1958

The Fayette County Hospital Board consisted of nine board members appointed by the Fayette County Commission for a term of six years each. Three members are appointed each year on a rotating basis with no limit to the number of terms a board member can serve. The hospital board has always included one member of the medical staff. A meeting was held to organize the Hospital Board on October 17, 1958, at the Chef Cafe located across from the livestock sale barn and adjoining Fowler Oil Company just north of Fayette. Herbert W. Matthews was elected chairman, H. C. Langston vice-chairman, and Gene S. Logan secretary-treasurer. Other appointed board members were Dr. B. W. McNease, Dr. J. D. Scrivner, Claude Campbell, Marvin T. Smith, Hollie M. Studdard, and Jonas D. Crawley. The Board adopted by-laws at this meeting. Shown below is a picture of the Fayette County Hospital Board taken in 1961.

Fayette County Hospital Board, 1961
Back L to R: J. D. Scrivner, Gene S. Logan, Marvin Smith, Jonas Crowley, and Robert Boone, Administrator; front L to R: Joe Posey Robertson, Claude Campbell, and Hollie Studdard. (Not shown: B. W. McNease).

The grand opening of Fayette County Hospital was held on Sunday September 21, 1958. Dedication ceremonies began at 2:00 p.m., followed by an open house so that everyone could see their new hospital and its equipment, because after it was in operation some areas would be restricted. Herbert Matthews, chairman of the hospital board, was master of ceremonies. The Fayette County High School Band, conducted by band director Jerry Bobo, presented a musical program. Rev. A. M. Nix, Pastor of First Baptist Church, gave the invocation. The welcome was given by Probate Judge Clyde C. Cargile. Dr. B. W. McNease introduced speakers, and Mayor Guthrie Smith introduced Congressman Carl Elliott as the main speaker. The benediction was given by Rev. O. G. Waid, Pastor of the First Methodist Church. The ribbon cutting was by Miss Neaten Perry, Fayette County Dairy Maid of Hubbertville. Everyone toured the new facility and was very impressed and excited about having such an up-to-date hospital. The proceedings went well, though some were concerned with the loudness of the band as it played in the hospital corridors. After the open house, Ms. May Caraway, reporting for Fayette's local paper, *The Broadcaster*, stated, "This community is richly blessed with some of the finest and most able men of the medical profession."

The new hospital had five doctors and 40 employees. The doctors were Dr. McNease, Dr. Hodo, Dr. Rutland, Dr. Fowler, and Dr. Scrivner. The employees went to work on Monday, September 22, 1958, to prepare for receiving patients. On September 24, 1958, four patients were transferred to the new hospital, three by car and one by ambulance because that patient required oxygen. On the same day, McNease-Hodo hospital was officially closed, but the doctors continued to maintain their offices and practices in the associated clinic where there were twelve examination rooms and an x-ray machine. After closing to in-patient care, the old hospital structure was renovated to create additional office and exam space for physicians. The new 35-bed Fayette County Hospital became a nucleus for further growth. In 1962, a 38-bed nursing home addition made the facility the Fayette County Hospital and Nursing Home. In 1996, as it continued to grow, the hospital was renamed Fayette Medical Center.

The Tradition of Quality
Care Continues...

The new Fayette County Hospital was very nice and equipped with the modern technology and instruments of that day. However, the work demands on the primary care doctors and their families were still very difficult. A typical day started around 7:00 a.m. with "morning rounds" to visit patients in the hospital. Next, the doctors took turns assisting Dr. Hodo as he performed surgery on their patients. Once the nursing home was added, the doctors' morning also included "nursing home rounds" to see patients and keep their charts properly recorded and up-to-date. There followed a full day in clinic with an average of 30 to 40 patients. All during the day it was necessary for them to interrupt clinic to respond to unscheduled phone calls from nurses reporting concerns for patients in the hospital and nursing home. The clinic schedule was maintained six days per week.

Each doctor took emergency room call every fourth day and was responsible for the care of patients who came to the Emergency Department. If stable, such patients were often referred to the doctor's clinic or held until the on-call doctor finished clinic and came to the Emergency Department to provide his services. If the patient was too ill for these protocols, the on-call doctor left the office and went to the emergency room to care for the patient. Obstetrical patients arriving for delivery provided another frequent interruption.

At about 6:00 p.m. each day, doctors returned to the hospital for "evening rounds" to visit critically ill patients and others whom they had admitted during the day from the clinic or Emergency Department. Following this, the on-call doctor attended to patients waiting in the emergency room, usually 20 or so. Finally, at the end of the hectic day, doctors went home, but rarely enjoyed a restful night.

Sleep was frequently interrupted by phone calls from nurses concerning patients in the hospital and nursing home. Expectant mothers always seemed to prefer nights to go into labor. The doctor on call often received calls from the emergency room nurse notifying him of the need to return to the hospital to care for a patient who was critically ill. When the Emergency Department was overwhelmed with multiple critically ill patients, such as from a car accident with multiple casualties, and exceeded the attending doctor's ability to care for them, the other physicians rallied to his support.

The physicians endured over a decade of this taxing practice before concurrent developments in medical education in the region began to supply some relief. In the late 1970s, the University of Alabama College of Community Health Sciences and associated Family Medicine Residency that Dr. Rutland was so instrumental in initiating came of age. Residents became available who were introduced to Fayette through Dr. Rutland's and other physicians' commitment to teaching. The Fayette physicians started paying interns and residents to come to Fayette on weekends to help see patients in their offices on Saturday. Then after clinic, the residents covered the emergency room on Saturday night and Sunday. This coverage was a great help to the local doctors, giving them a break from what was referred to as "first call." After what was typically a tough weekend of practical experience of moonlighting for the residents, Dr. Rutland and Mrs. Nancy usually invited the young doctors over to their house for a delicious meal before seeing them return to their formal training in Tuscaloosa.

During these difficult times, the doctors had a very special helper, relieving them of much of the burden required in the care of obstetric patients. Mrs. Lovie Maddox Oswalt, a life-long, beloved resident of Fayette County (September 7, 1907-November 2, 1985), was a practicing midwife and the last of the independent practicing midwives. She was one of 12 children and married Alsie Lee Oswalt. She was a member of Oak Grove Methodist Church and was a special person. Her work was a labor of love and more of a mission than a job. She went into very low income living conditions to assist mothers who had no other option. She assisted in the delivery of babies during the early 1940s and during World War II. She delivered her first baby alone on May 29, 1954, and assisted in over 1,000 deliveries until July 5, 1978. She often brought her expectant mothers to the Department of Public Health, located across the street from the doctors' clinic, and the doctors walked over to see the mothers. Mrs. Oswalt had a good sense of when the mother was in trouble and, when this occurred, she took the mother to the hospital for assistance. Mrs. Oswalt never lost a baby or mother.

In 1987, the doctors stopped delivering babies at Fayette County Hospital. Two factors were influential to this decision. One was that malpractice insurance costs had become outrageously expensive, beyond the family doctors' reach. The other was an evolving demand from expectant mothers for birthing rooms, an accommodation that the hospital could not afford to make.

The hospital and physicians' practices continued to adapt and change with the opportunities and constraints of the times. One improvement in the hospital was the pharmacy. Initially, Neal Meherg, the purchasing agent, secured all the drugs and maintained them in general storage. Nurses requisitioned drugs, as needed, to their drug room and dispensed them to patients per doctors' orders. After a few years, Julian McGuire, a part-time pharmacist, was contracted to oversee all processes pertaining to handling of medications. Several years after the new hospital opened, Mrs. Pat McCrackin, a full-time pharmacist, was employed. At first, she was allocated the nurses' medicine room, no larger than a good-sized closet, to house the pharmacy. She convinced administration to install a sink in this small room. But Pat never complained. She just did such a good job that the department outgrew this location and had to be moved to a larger space.

In 1979, the McNease doctor group moved their practice to a new building they had constructed across the highway from the hospital. At the reception to mark the opening of the new clinical site, Dr. Hodo was honored for his many years of dedicated service. The honor included formally naming the new building the McNease-Hodo Clinic. At that time, all the doctors belonged to one group, and the group felt a responsibility to care for all patients in the area regardless of their ability to pay.

After the doctor group moved to their new building, the doctors sold the downtown clinic to the county for much needed office and parking space. The building was appraised for $266,000, but the civic-minded doctors sold it to the city government for $125,000. The first tenant in the now public building was the Fayette County Department of Human Resources, which remained there until early 2000 when its own new building was ready.

In May 2000, the old McNease clinic building was torn down due to severe structural problems. Unfortunately, the "Champion" oak tree, so designated because it was the largest representation of its species in Alabama, in back of the clinic was cut down at this same time. The State Department of Public Health constructed a new Public Health building, which was a fitting successor to the property where Dr. McNease had started the clinical practice that had meant so much to the health of Fayette and the surrounding area. The window shown here was removed from the clinic when it was torn down. It has a brief historical account of medical care in the county in three of the window panes and is on display at Fayette

Medical Center. The McNease, Robertson, Hodo clinic-hospital is no longer standing but the tradition of quality health care in Fayette County continues.

Window with history from the original McNease-Hodo Clinic

Perhaps this structural artifact is a fitting reminder of the influence of the medical profession that Fayette County has enjoyed for nearly a century, dating back to Dr. McNease's arrival in 1926. As a rule, the medical professionals of Fayette have conducted themselves with a passion for their role that has consistently raised the bar of expectations for medical care. Fayette County is proud of this history of quality health care. However, the urge to excellence was not limited to the clinic or the hospital.

Fayette physicians and administrators have extended this influence to larger venues. Dr. Banks Robertson, Mr. Robert Boone, and Mr. Barry Cochran served as chairmen of the Alabama Hospital Association. Dr. Henry Hodo, Dr. Richard Rutland, Mr. Robert Boone, and Mr. Barry Cochran have served on the Blue Cross Blue Shield Board of Directors. Dr. B. W. McNease and Dr. Jon Sanford served in the prestigious position of president of the Medical Association of the State of Alabama. Dr. Richard Rutland and Dr. Gary Magouirk have been presidents of the Alabama Academy of Family Physicians. Through the years, other administrators and physicians have served in a variety of important positions as well.

But even as Fayette has exercised an expanding influence throughout the region, it has had to adapt to the changing health care environment brought about by advances in the science, technology, and costs of medicine. The early 1980s brought changes in health policies aimed at curbing rising health care costs. Small rural hospitals around the country felt the effects of these changes most acutely because the populations they served were not large enough to create the economies of scale needed to survive within the razor thin operating margins that sustained them. One cost-containing policy was Medicare's implementation of the diagnostic-related group (DRG) payment system. This policy limited payment for care of patients with similar diagnoses to an average reimbursement without regard for the variation in severity of illness that might occur within the group. Thus, one severely ill patient might consume the medical attention and resources required for ten mildly ill patients, but the reimbursement was the same. Large hospitals serving expansive populations could create operating margins from the care of many mildly ill patients sufficient to cover the extra care required by the severely ill. Small rural hospitals could not. Due to this change, it became very difficult for any small hospital in Alabama to survive without an affiliation with a tertiary referral hospital. Alabama led the nation in the 1980s in the rate of rural hospital closures.

In Fayette, the process of dealing with this reality was not straightforward. There was a long period of differing opinions among the hospital board, county commission, and medical staff. Each had legitimate reason to claim some authority in the determination of who could enter into an affiliation agreement with a larger medical facility. The matter was carried to district court, which clarified

> *"By necessity, this Order has vested ownership of the Hospital in the Hospital Board, but that ownership is for control purposes alone and is in trust for the citizens of this county. The citizens of Fayette County are the true owners of the hospital regardless of who has control and that should not be forgotten by those in control".*

To stabilize the financial position of Fayette County Hospital and Nursing Home, on August 16, 1984, the board signed a management agreement with DCH

Healthcare System in Tuscaloosa, but retained ownership of the facility. With the security of membership in a larger system, there was also modification in the degree to which the local medical profession and community could impact their system of care.

The Transition

Much is said today (2014) about the business of medicine, health care management and administration, and health care policy. Less is heard about medical authority and the profession of medicine. There has been a shift in emphasis with concern for costs, standardization, and accountability based on business principles more than on the patient-physician relationship. The honored profession with inherent checks and balances is often viewed as a pathway to economic prestige and status, rather than one of humble service. Medicine has become "the health care industry" encompassing medical care along with a host of connected services and technologies. For example, there are pharmacies, assistive equipment, medical transportation, home health care, and assisted living, to name a few. Insurance programs and managed care are dominant themes.

In today's health care industry, a transition has occurred in the way medicine is practiced. Very few modern physicians want day after day of practice like Dr. Hodo endured, leaving home at five-thirty a.m. with the goal of getting home for dinner by ten p.m. in mind. However, they do have new issues that are mentally and emotionally distressing, which earlier doctors never had to consider. After all, it is a different world entirely in which they practice.

Dr. Henry Hodo, in reference to Dr. McNease, quoted Ben Franklin as saying, "In darkness as in light our responsibilities are with us." Then Dr. Hodo said, "It was this sense of duty and responsibility for the health care of the people of this area that prompted Dr. B. W. McNease to build a clinic and a hospital." Dr. McNease saw patients in his home, like most doctors of his time. Dr. McNease did not find it necessary or more convenient to construct an $11,000 clinic in 1936; it was about having x-ray and other modern equipment available for the patients and improving the quality of health care. When Dr. McNease and Dr. Robertson built the hospital, it was not about making their practice easier, for it added to their responsibility. It was about not having to send patients to Jasper or Tuscaloosa to be admitted to a hospital. It was about patients being able to have emergency surgery without riding the train to Jasper. It was all about caring for the patients and improving the quality of their care and lives.

This practice of medicine in early years had it challenges, but it had some advantages, also. Dr. Hodo said, "The family doctor was not only the healer of sickness, but also a confidante, trusted friend, sounding board and problem solver for many things not related to a person's physical well-being." The doctor was trusted as both healer and friend of the patient. This relationship fueled the seemingly endless devotion of the physicians. The practice of medicine in years gone by was very physically demanding with long, tiring days; large patient loads; and very poor travel conditions. However, the early doctors were not overwhelmed with issues that consume physicians today. Today's practice is still physically demanding, but not as mentally draining. The practice of today is emotionally exhausting and strenuous. Today's doctors are faced with bureaucratic concerns and the tedium of multiple forms of paperwork and computer input. There are Center for Medical Services (CMS) regulations, accreditation standards, licensing requirements, liability concerns, and certification/re-certification requirements. The new CMS requirement for doctors to make their own computer order entries is very burdensome and time consuming. Most physicians consider it to be foolish, taking them away from the patient to do clerical work.

Family physicians, the most common type of doctor in Fayette, make their livelihood primarily through their office practice. Cost-containing reimbursement policies and inefficiencies brought about by bureaucratic requirements make this a low profit margin proposition. Thus, having to miss lunch or, even worse, to break from clinical practice to attend an issue in the hospital creates additional financial distress. Such situations are forcing many doctors to limit or curtail hospital practice, just as in days gone by when they limited obstetrical care because of the unreasonable costs of associated professional liability insurance. Perhaps there is some irony in the fact that doctors today may find it more functional to conduct a clinic-based practice similar to that of Dr. McNease prior to his guidance of Fayette medicine toward a hospital-centered system. Consequently, the hospital faces uncertainty.

There is no mistaking the impact that social, economic, and demographic forces are having on the health care system today. There must be enough patients, financial support, physicians, support personnel, and administration to sustain a small hospital. As local economies have contracted in response to global patterns such as closure of the coal mine as oil has become less expensive and the loss of textile industry to cheaper workforces overseas, the population has ceased to expand and the local financial base has been compromised. There are fewer insured patients with many younger individuals leaving the area to join the workforce. The local population is aging both by longevity and by loss of young people, creating additional stress on the health care system with this greater associated burden of illness. The prominence of high tech and specialty-based medicine made glamorous and lucrative in our society has created an exodus of young people in pursuit of medical careers based on those impressions. The generalist physicians that characterize those who established Fayette as a center of excellence in rural health care are in exceedingly short supply. The physicians who do commit to practice in areas such as Fayette today are very special.

Fayette is situated in West Alabama, which experiences a regional economy suppressed below that of the remainder of the state and most of the nation. It is little wonder that in this region there is strain among relationships between hospitals and doctors. However, it has been in times of such stress that finding common cause and sense of purpose has sustained the health care system. In the 1970s, following a period of severe shortage of primary care physicians, the College of Community Health Sciences (CCHS) was started at The University of Alabama with Dr. Richard Rutland playing a large part. That effort required cooperation and helping each other, a circumstance that continued to exist for a decade. Then in the 1980s, a nationwide depression in the rural economy greatly stressed Alabama, and many rural hospitals closed their doors never to reopen. The concurrent economic attractiveness of cities and specialty medicine prolonged the plight of struggling rural hospitals as young physicians sought urban practices. Alabama declared a rural health crisis in 1989, which again signaled the need for cooperative actions. In West Alabama, Fayette leaders joined others from surrounding counties and from CCHS to organize the Rural Alabama Health Alliance (RAHA), a nonprofit organization that created an environment of trust, corporation, and support among the groups representing each member county. Representatives included physicians, hospital administrators, and other citizens. Dr. Garry Magouirk and Mr. Harold Reed were constant representatives from Fayette. A closer relationship among the counties and the medical training programs of CCHS resulted, which eventuated in a more stable supply of local physicians in member counties.

Now the problems of not knowing what the future holds and mistrust, especially among hospital and medical staffs, again have created a very stressful environment. The survival of individual doctors' practices and of rural hospitals is at stake. In rural communities such as Fayette, where sources of employment are limited, the local hospital provides both health care and economic stability. Everyone must pull together in support of their hospital to keep it viable. The loss of a hospital has a disastrous effect on these communities. Not long after Fayette County Hospital was built, the local economy experienced a downturn. Patients would often tell their doctor that they did not have enough money to pay their bill. The doctors, knowing how important the hospital was, would tell their patients, "You pay your hospital bill and you can pay me later." While physicians may not enjoy the same financial security today as in those days, the same spirit of common cause among the community, physicians, and hospital leadership is needed for hospital survival and for a wholesome community.

There is general agreement that medicine is different today than in years past. There are many factors involved, such as changes in training with decreased duty hours, more gender equality in medicine, more employed practices vs. private practice, less autonomy, and less professional influence on health policy. Today's doctors require more time with their family, which is good for the doctors and their families. Due to the stress of the profession, the doctor needs more time away from career demands. However, doctors still face the need to balance their time demands. To be a good family doctor, one is expected to be a good member of the community and to be aware of the issues one's patients are facing. Due to the conflict in the amount of time the doctor has to devote to his profession and the amount of time he feels he has available, most young doctors don't get active in professional organizations. They find it enough to carve out time needed to meet their mandated continuing education requirements.

Although the group practice started by Dr. McNease ended in 1990, the doctors in Fayette have continued in a cooperative working relationship. While their practice styles may differ, they each accept responsibility on the medical staff and are very supportive of the hospital.

Garry Magouirk, MD

Family Practice

Dr. Magouirk was born in Anniston, Alabama, but grew up in the small community of Ohatchee, population of

700, in Northeast Alabama. He attended Ohatchee High School where he played on the football, baseball, and track teams. Dr. Magouirk attended Gadsden State Community College for two years.

While in community college, Dr. Magouirk decided he would pursue

Garry Magouirk, MD

a career as a family doctor. He transferred to Auburn University where after two years he received a Bachelors of Science degree in Chemistry. He then entered the University of Alabama School of Medicine (UASOM) at the University of Alabama at Birmingham. He completed the two years of pre-clinical sciences in Birmingham, and chose to complete the clinical third and fourth years on the UASOM branch campus in Tuscaloosa with its appeal to students preparing for primary care medical careers, particularly in rural Alabama. This branch campus was housed in the University of Alabama College of Community Health Sciences, which Dr. Richard Rutland had been instrumental in helping to develop. Dr. Magouirk received the Doctor of Medicine degree in 1980.

He stayed in Tuscaloosa for another three years to complete training for family practice at the Tuscaloosa Family Practice Residency. Again, this residency was the program for which Dr. Rutland served as initial director, placing it on firm footing. During the first year of his residency Dr. Magouirk met and married Janice Hamlin.

While Dr. Magouirk was in residency, he was contacted by Brother Byron White, a Methodist minister, about practicing in Berry, Alabama, a small town in southeast Fayette County. Brother White has been the Minister at the First United Methodist Church back in Ohatchee and had known Garry as he was growing up. When Brother White relocated his ministry to Berry, he found that Berry was without a physician and soon became the chairman of a search committee to find the community a doctor. He immediately thought of Dr. Magouirk, who was still in training.

To recruit Dr. Magouirk, Berry agreed to help him financially with the expense of medical education, and he agreed to practice in the town of Berry for four years. In preparation for Dr. Magouirk, Brother White worked diligently in the community and was able to have a clinic building constructed. While still in residency, Dr. Magouirk began to involve himself in the community by attending the high school football games and serving as team physician. When he completed his residency in Family Medicine in 1983, he immediately came to Berry and started practice.

Dr. Magouirk found that Berry was too small a community to support a full-scale family medicine practice. He began to work at the Fayette County Hospital Emergency Department taking two day shifts every other weekend and one night shift each week to supplement his income. However, he and Berry came to realize that he would need to locate in nearby Fayette to sustain a practice that could still serve Berry. While continuing to live in Berry, he moved his practice to Fayette in the McNease-Hodo clinic in 1986. He stayed in that location for three years. In 1989, Dr. Magouirk purchased a clinic being vacated of Dr. Phil Smith who was moving from Fayette.

In 1986, Dr. Magouirk accepted responsibility for coordinating the staffing of the Emergency Department (ED) during nights and on weekends using second and third year residents in the Tuscaloosa Family Practice Residency Program. This was a great relief to the doctors on staff at Fayette County Hospital who were taking turns in covering the ED. However, in time, the residents began working less and less, and Dr. Magouirk was responsible in their absence, sometimes working three consecutive 24-hour shifts. This occurred too often, and Dr. Magourik employed Dr. Bob Grubbs to work days in the ED, making it feasible for Dr. Magouirk to service a contract covering the ED 24 hours per day and seven days per week. This worked well for four years until Dr. Grubbs moved back to Tuscaloosa. Dr. Magouirk gave up his contract at that time, and the hospital entered into a contract with an agency that provided emergency medicine coverage.

During Dr. Magouirk's years of practice, he has served in several positions in the Fayette County Hospital Medical Staff, including chairman of the Emergency Department Committee, member of Quality Assurance Committee, and president of Medical Staff. He held other positions outside the hospital, which included

- Member of the Alabama Academy of Family Physicians, serving as president, 1995-96.
- Alabama Delegate to the American Academy of Family Physicians.
- Member of UAB School of Medicine Admissions Committee.
- Member of the Alabama Family Practice Rural Health Board.
- Preceptor for College of Community Health Sciences, 1983 to present.
- Rural Alabama Health Alliance, including all leadership positions.

Dr. Magouirk was an original member of the Rural Alabama Health Alliance (RAHA), which was formed in 1990 as a 501.3.c non-profit organization to bring rural community voice to the policy processes affecting medical education. RAHA was composed predominantly of members of Fayette County, Pickens

County, Bibb County, and the University of Alabama College of Community Health Sciences Rural Health Programs. Dr. John Wheat, a faculty member with the Rural Health Programs, served as staff assistant to the RAHA board. Dr. Magouirk served at various times as secretary, vice-chair, and chairman of the RAHA board. As an officer, he helped to formalize the development of a required rural rotation for Tuscaloosa Family Practice Residency Program residents in the RAHA counties, including Fayette. Combining his work with RAHA and the Alabama Academy of Family Physicians, he was an influential voice in guiding the University of Alabama School of Medicine to create the Rural Medical Scholars Program (RMSP) at the UA College of Community Health Sciences. This program has begun to fulfill its potential to produce needed physicians for rural Alabama. Several students from the Fayette area have participated, and neighboring Pickens County has three family physicians trained through the RMSP.

Dr. Magouirk made Berry, Alabama his home and has maintained an active presence in the community. He and his family are in regular attendance at the First United Methodist Church in Berry, where he has served as the chairman of the Administrative Council. Janice Magouirk became a teacher in Berry, where Dr. Magouirk is the team physician. They had two children, a daughter and son. His daughter explored the idea of following her father's footsteps by participating in the University of Alabama Rural Health Scholars Program in the summer after her junior year of high school. She was able to consider the idea of a medical career, but found that this was not her calling.

Dr. Magouirk has built a large, busy practice, composed of patients from Berry and Fayette. He is loved and respected in the community and by his patients. In recent years, he has limited his hospital practice, but continues his clinical practice in the same location where he has been for 34 years. Since 2000, he has been joined in practice by Dr. Gregory Stidham and Nurse Practitioner Hillary Gant.

John E. Morrison, MD
Janice L. Hudson, MD

General Surgery   Family Practice

The professional couple of Dr. Janice Hudson and Dr. John Morrison made a significant contribution to the hospital and community during their 20-year practice in Fayette. They were exceptionally well trained at Louisiana State University (LSU), and each achieved board certification, she in family medicine and he in surgery. They left New Roads, Louisiana, and arrived in Fayette in 1987, practicing in Fayette until 2007. Their daughter, Sigourney ("Signey"), was only two years old when they arrived in Fayette. As a result, Dr. Hudson delayed a few months in starting her practice.

John E. Morrison, MD

Janice Hudson, MD

Dr. Hudson proved to be an excellent clinician and developed a large practice. She was trusted and loved by her patients. A common sentiment was "Dr. Hudson will find out what is wrong with you." Beyond clinical care, she was active in supporting the hospital. She served on the Executive Committee, was chairman of the Medical Records Committee, and was president of the Medical Staff for one term. It was a sad day for Fayette when Dr. Hudson closed her practice. She has been missed greatly.

Dr. Morrison was an exceptionally skilled surgeon, which he credited to his residency at LSU's Charity Hospital in New Orleans where he performed an extremely large number of surgery cases. He was an innovator, becoming among the first surgeons to learn and perfect the use of laparoscopic surgery. He demonstrated a scholarly approach to practicing surgery, carrying on the tradition of high quality, science-based health care established in Fayette first by Dr. B. W. McNease. He effectively adapted Fayette County Hospital to be not only a place of surgical care, but also a clinical research and teaching facility for modern surgical therapeutics. While at Fayette, he implemented and modified several laparoscopic procedures. His most noteworthy was the Classic Intrafascial Supracervical Hysterectomy (CISH) procedure, a laparoscopy hysterectomy done as an outpatient procedure. A clinical scholar, he authored or co-authored more than 20 articles in scientific publications, as listed below, based on his work in Fayette.

Scientific Articles by John E. Morrison, Jr., M.D.

Jacobs VR, Morrison JE. Comparison of institutional costs for laparoscopic preperitoneal inguinal hernia versus open repair and its reimbursement in an ambulatory surgery center. *Surg Laparosc Endosc Percutan Tech.* 2008 Feb;18(1):70-4.

Morrison JE, Jacobs VR. Laparoscopic preperitoneal inguinal hernia repair using preformed polyester mesh without fixation: prospective study with 1-year follow-up results in a rural setting. *Surg Laparosc Endosc Percutan Tech.* 2008 Feb;18(1):33-9.

Morrison JE, Jacobs VR. Rupture of the spleen with the harmonic scalpel: case report of an unexplained complication. *JSLS.* 2007 Apr-Jun;11(2):268-71.

Jacobs VR, Morrison JE. Application of a locally placed anesthesia catheter for reduction of postoperative pain after mastectomy for breast cancer. *Int J Fertil Womens Med.* 2006 Sep-Oct;51(5):225-9.

Jacobs VR, Morrison JE. The real intraabdominal pressure during laparoscopy: comparison of different insufflators. *J Minim Invasive Gynecol.* 2007 Jan-Feb;14(1):103-7.

Morrison JE, Jacobs VR. Classic Intrafascial Supracervical Hysterectomy (CISH): 10-year experience. *Journal of the Society of Laparoendoscopic Surgeons* 2006 Jan-Mar; 10(1): 26–29.

Jacobs VR, Morrison JE, Paepke S, Fischer T, Kiechle M. Three-dimensional model for gas flow, resistance, and leakage-dependent nominal pressure maintenance of different laparoscopic insufflators. *J Minim Invasive Gynecol.* 2006 May-Jun;13(3):225-30.

Jacobs VR, Kiechle M, Morrison JE. Carbon dioxide gas heating inside laparoscopic insufflators has no effect. *JSLS.* 2005 Apr-Jun;9(2):208-12.

Jacobs VR, Morrison JE, Paepke S, Kiechle M. Body piercing affecting laparoscopy: perioperative precautions. *J Am Assoc Gynecol Laparosc.* 2004 Nov;11(4):537-41.

Jacobs VR, Morrison JE, Kiechle M. Twenty-five simple ways to increase insufflation performance and patient safety in laparoscopy. *J Am Assoc Gynecol Laparosc.* 2004 Aug;11(3):410-23.

Morrison JE, Jacobs VR. Outpatient laparoscopic hysterectomy in a rural ambulatory surgery center. *J Am Assoc Gynecol Laparosc.* 2004 Aug;11(3):359-64.

Morrison JE, Jacobs VR. Replacement of expensive, disposable instruments with old-fashioned surgical techniques for improved cost-effectiveness in laparoscopic hysterectomy. *JSLS.* 2004 Apr-Jun;8(2):201-6.

Morrison JE, Jacobs VR. Reduction or elimination of postoperative pain medication after mastectomy through use of a temporarily placed local anesthetic pump vs. control group. *Zentralbl Gynakol.* 2003 Jan;125(1):17-22.

Jacobs VR, Morrison JE. Warmed insufflation carbon dioxide gas for laparoscopic cholecystectomy. *Surg Endosc.* 2001 Oct;15(10):1244-5. No abstract available.

Morrison JE, Jacobs VR. 437 classic intrafascial supracervical hysterectomies in 8 years. *J Am Assoc Gynecol Laparosc.* 2001 Nov;8(4):558-67.

Jacobs VR, Morrison JE, Mundhenke C, Golombeck K, Jonat W. Intraoperative evaluation of laparoscopic insufflation technique for quality control in the OR. *JSLS.* 2000 Jul-Sep;4(3):189-95.

Jacobs VR, Morrison JE, Mundhenke C, Golombeck K, Jonat W, Harder D. Model to determine resistance and leakage-dependent flow on flow performance of laparoscopic insufflators to predict gas flow rate of cannulas. *J Am Assoc Gynecol Laparosc.* 2000 Aug;7(3):331-7.

Jacobs VR, Morrison JE, Mettler L, Mundhenke C, Jonat W. Measurement of CO(2) hypothermia during laparoscopy and pelviscopy: how cold it gets and how to prevent it. *J Am Assoc Gynecol Laparosc.* 1999 Aug;6(3):289-95.
Morrison JE, Jacobs VR. Re: Videothorascopic removal of a mediastinal teratoma. *Am Surg.* 1998 Sep;64(9):912. Morrison JE, Jacobs VR. Laparoscopy-assisted endoscopic bowel anastomosis stenosis revision with stapler: report of two cases. *Surg Laparosc Endosc.* 1998 Jun;8(3):211-4.

Jacobs VR, Morrison JE. Computer in the O.R. for quality control. Intraoperative data acquisition model for laparoscopy. *Stud Health Technol Inform.* 1998;50: 359-60.

Dr. Morrison received national recognition for his scientific contributions. Over the years, Dr. Morrison made numerous oral scientific presentations and displayed posters at medical meetings worldwide. He received several awards from medical societies, among them the prestigious Kurt-Semm Award for Excellence in Pelviscopy by the American Association of Gynecologic Laparoscopists (AAGL) at their 1998 congress in Atlanta. This award was named after the inventor and developer of operative laparoscopy, Prof. Dr. Kurt Seem from Kiel, Germany. For a time, Dr. Volker R. Jacobs from Germany stayed in Fayette to collaborate with Dr. Morrison and publish the research work on the CISH and other laparoscopic modalities. Dr. Morrison's CISH procedure attracted the attention of Ethicon, a surgical supply company, which arranged for Dr. Morrison to do a video conference from the Fayette Medical Center operating room to a general audience of national and international physicians at a convention in Los Angeles, California. It was reported that his laparoscopic hysterectomy procedure went so quickly, taking just half of the expected time, that congress attendees had to hurry back from the coffee break to not miss the finish of this highly professional procedure.

Dr. Morrison was a remarkable surgeon. His innovations reduced the invasiveness of surgery and the intensity and complications of surgical care. Hysterectomies could be done as outpatient procedures. Consequently, he was in great demand for surgical care and as a speaker at professional societies. His large general surgery practice was very supportive of the hospital. Combined with primary care provided by the stable group of family physicians in the community, all but the most severe medical conditions could be handled in Fayette. During the time he practiced in Fayette, he was chairman of the Surgery Committee. He also served on the Medical Staff Quality Assurance Committee and the Hospital Executive Committee. He was president of the Medical Staff for two terms. He served Fayette as delegate to the Medical Association of the State of Alabama, 1991-1998. Also, he was a reviewer for several scientific surgical journals.

Dr. Hudson and Dr. Morrison regularly attended the First United Methodist Church and were highly regarded leaders in the community. They received the Chamber of Commerce "Man and Woman of the Year" award. Drs. Hudson and Morrison enjoyed their time in Fayette. However, Dr. Morrison's scholarly work caught the attention of academic medicine and he was offered the opportunity to return to New Orleans, his hometown, and LSU, his alma mater, to teach medical students and surgery residents. He became head of the Department of Minimally Invasive Surgery and director of the Surgery Residency. The Fayette community was very proud to have Dr. Morrison and Dr. Hudson for the twenty years they were there.

Charles W. Nolen, Jr., MD, JD

General Practice

Charles W. Nolen, Jr., MD, JD was born at Fayette County Hospital and raised in Fayette, Alabama, the son of Charles W. Nolen, Sr., JD, a well-known and respected attorney in the community. He competed as a member of the track team and graduated from Fayette County High School in 1976 in the top ten of his class. Dr. Nolen went to Tuscaloosa and attended The University of Alabama, where he completed the undergraduate degree with a major in History and a minor in Biology. He desired to become a physician, motivated strongly through the

influence of Dr. Breitling. But while he was completing college, Dr. Nolen's father was very sick, and he felt he should continue the family business. So he remained in Tuscaloosa and entered the University of Alabama School of Law and earned the Juris Doctor degree in 1983.

Charles W. Nolen, Jr., M.D., JD

While Dr. Nolen was still in law school, his father's health improved, and Dr. Nolen decided to follow his true desire to become a doctor. While in law school, he took chemistry classes to prepare for medical school. One month after completing law school, Dr. Nolen started medical school. He went to the University of Alabama at Birmingham (UAB) School of Medicine. In the first year of medical school, Dr. Nolen married Bonita, and they later had three children. Dr. Nolen did his Family Medicine rotation with Dr. Breitling in Fayette. He received the Doctor of Medicine degree in 1987.

Dr. Nolen took an internship in internal medicine at the Quillen-Dishner (now James H. Quillen) College of Medicine in Johnson City, Tennessee. After internship, Dr. Nolen went to Carraway Burdick-West Memorial Hospital in Haleyville, Alabama, where he worked as the Emergency Department physician for one year. Then he came home to Fayette in 1990, where he has practiced for 23 years. Dr. Nolen maintained an active hospital practice until 2000. As to why he stopped working at the hospital, he reported that he loved his hospital practice and being around all the nurses and hospital staff, "but the bureaucracy and red tape just became too much."

Dr. Nolen maintains an active practice and is appreciated by his patients. His professional involvement includes memberships in the American Medical Association and the American College of Legal Medicine. He has membership in other organizations related to his expertise as a pilot.

Dr. Nolen is active in the community. He is a member of the Fayette Area Chamber of Commerce and active in the Fayette First Baptist Church, where he serves as a deacon and Sunday School teacher. Also, Bonita and their son play in the church orchestra.

Frederick Yerby, MD

Family Practice

Frederick Yerby, MD was delivered at Fayette County Hospital in 1963 (by Dr. Rutland) and raised in Fayette, Alabama. Dr. Yerby graduated from Fayette County High School where he played in the high school band and was valedictorian of his graduating class. Dr. Yerby said Mr. Hooker, his high school Biology and Human Anatomy teacher, was very influential in his becoming a doctor. He was also influenced toward medicine by Miss Brock, a Biology teacher and sister-in-law of Dr. Hodo, and by Dr. Harold Breitling.

He attended The University of Alabama in Tuscaloosa and graduated with the Bachelors of Science degree majoring in Chemistry in December 1984. Similar to Dr. Magouirk, he benefitted from Dr. Rutland's work to help establish the branch medical education program and family medicine residency in Tuscaloosa; he attended the University of Alabama School of Medicine at Birmingham (UAB) for the two pre-clinical years of medical school, but returned to the College of Community

Health Sciences in Tuscaloosa for the clinical years. He was awarded the Doctor of Medicine degree in 1989. He remained in Tuscaloosa to complete the family medicine residency and became board certified.

Frederick Yerby, MD

In 1992, Dr. Yerby returned home to Fayette and established a family medicine practice where he has practiced continuously for 21 years. During this time, he has carried on the tradition of supporting Fayette Medical Center and the medical staff. He has served as president of the medical staff for three terms and on medical staff committees including the Executive Committee.

Dr. Yerby participates in professional associations and in support of medical education. These activities include

- 1992 to present Member of the Alabama Academy of Family Physicians.
- 1992 to present Member of the American Academy of Family Physicians.
- 1996 Fellow in the American Academy of Family Physicians.

- 2011 Member of the Board of Visitors of the College of Community Health Sciences.

Debbie Kilgore was practicing pharmacy in Berry, Alabama at the time that Dr. Yerby entered practice in nearby Fayette. She and Dr. Yerby became acquainted as Dr. Yerby called in prescriptions for his patients who lived in the Berry area. In December 1994, they were married and have become the parents of four children. Dr. Yerby is a family man who also likes to hunt and fish. He is a faithful supporter of the community. He volunteers his time as the Fayette County High School football team doctor. He is highly involved with his children and their sports and attends their games regularly. Dr. Yerby is a faithful member of the Belk Freewill Baptist Church.

Martha Jo Christian, M.D.

Internal Medicine

Martha Jo Christian was born in Fayette County hospital and was raised in Fayette, Alabama. Her father, Mr. Lynnwood Christian, was Director of the Laboratory Department at Fayette County Hospital for 39 years. Dr. Christian said she grew up in the halls of Fayette County Hospital and her father had a great influence on her becoming a doctor. She was often in the hospital and observed the doctors, nurses, and other medical personnel going about their work, which made her want to go into medicine. One day she was riding with her father in his red pickup truck and she told him she wanted to work in the laboratory like him. He quickly corrected her and said, "You don't want a career in lab work." She replied, "Okay, I will be a nurse." Her father said, "If you are going into a career in medicine, you can only be a doctor or a hospital administrator." Dr. Christian chose to become a doctor.

Martha Jo Christian, MD

Dr. Christian was a very bright student. She attended Fayette County High School and was valedictorian of her class. She played in the high school band throughout her high school years. After high school, she attended Birmingham Southern University where in 1992 she graduated magna cum laude with a degree in Chemistry. While at Birmingham Southern she was a member of Phi Delta Kappa, an association for professional educators "to grow and connect leaders in education." She also participated in the Student Government Association (SGA) and was editor of the *Hilltop News*, the official student newspaper of Birmingham Southern.

She stayed in Birmingham and received her Doctor of Medicine degree in 1996 from the University of Alabama at Birmingham (UAB) School of Medicine She remained at UAB for three years and completed residency training in the Internal Medicine-Primary Care Track in 1999.

Dr. Christian entered solo practice in Fayette in

August of 1999, which she has continued for 14 years. Dr. Christian said that she was very proud to be following great physicians like Drs. B. W. McNease, John Banks Robertson, Henry Gunter Hodo, and Richard O. Rutland and to be carrying on the tradition of quality health care that these doctors had established.

Dr. Christian is board certified by the American Board of Internal Medicine. She has a very active practice and is a strong supporter of the hospital and medical staff. She served two terms as president of the Medical Staff and has been chairman of the Medical Staff Quality Assurance Committee. She serves on the Pharmacy and Therapeutics Committee, the Medical Records Committee, and Ethics Committee. Her professional interests extend to membership in medical associations. She is a member of the American College of Physicians and of the Medical Association of the State of Alabama.

In 2001, Dr. Christian married Ward Pierce and they have three children. Ward is a nurse and works for a doctor in Jasper, Alabama. Dr. Christian is very active in the community. She has been a member of Fayette Area Chamber of Commerce since 1999. She attends the First Baptist Church of Fayette where she is active with the music program. She is an accomplished pianist, routinely playing for church services. She participates in church orchestra, choir, and children's choir and has served on the Music and Community Service committees.

Dr. Martha Jo Christian is a very loving and caring person. She is devoted to the medical profession, the community, and her patients.

Gregory Paul Stidham, M.D.

Family Practice

Gregory Paul Stidham was raised in the small rural community of Hodges in Franklin County in the northwest corner of Alabama. Dr. Stidham was the second of three children. He attended Hackleburg High School in Hackleburg, Alabama, about five miles from Hodges. He graduated in 1988 and was valedictorian of his class. He played on the high school basketball team, where Coach Ronnie Anglin was most influential in his decision to become a doctor.

After high school, Dr. Stidham attended the Northwest Alabama Community College in Phil Campbell, Alabama and in 1990 graduated with an Associate in Science degree. He then attended the University of Alabama at Birmingham (UAB), graduating in 1992 with a Bachelor of Science with a major in Biology and minor

Gregory P. Stidham, MD

in Chemistry. He next attended the University of South Alabama College of Medicine in Mobile, Alabama, where in 1997 he received his Doctor of Medicine degree. Dr. Stidham made his final educational move to the College of Community Health Science at The University of Alabama in Tuscaloosa, Alabama, where he completed three years of family practice residency in 2000.

Since 2000, Dr. Stidham has practiced in association with Dr. Garry Magouirk in Fayette, which is only about one hour south of Dr. Stidham's home town of Hodges. He is highly respected and considered an excellent physician by the community,

As well as his outpatient practice, Dr. Stidham is active on the Fayette Medical Center Medical Staff through which the hospital derives support from his very active practice. He has served on the Executive Committee and has been president of the Medical Staff for three terms. He has been chairman of the Health Information Management Committee and chairman of the Emergency Department Committee.

Dr. Stidham maintains current affiliation with his professional associations. Since 2000, he has been a member of the Fayette County Medical Society, Medical Association of the State of Alabama, and the American Academy of Family Physicians.

Dr. Stidham is active in the community. He married Dana Gober and they have four children, three boys and girl. Dr. Stidham and his family are in regular attendance at the First Baptist Church of Fayette. He is the team physician for the Hubbertville High School and Junior

High football teams, attending all games for both teams. The boys are active in sports.

Gabe Stidham, Dr. Stidham's oldest child, plans at this stage in his life to follow his father's footsteps into medicine. In the summer after his eleventh grade year, he attended the UA College of Community Health Sciences' Rural Health Scholars Program and plans to be a UA Rural Medical Scholar to prepare for practice in rural medicine. These rural programs in the College of Community Health Sciences extend the college's mission of producing rural physicians. They resulted, in part, from the efforts of Dr. Rutland to help initiate and stabilize the College and Dr. Garry Magouirk's and Mr. Harold Reed's work through the Rural Alabama Health Alliance to guide the College's outreach programs.

Jonathan Smith, MD

General Surgery

Dr. Jonathan Smith was born in Haleyville, less than an hour's drive from Fayette. He grew up both in Haleyville and Huntsville. He played football and basketball in high school and ran cross-country in college.

Jonathan was greatly influenced to become a doctor by two physicians during his formative years. The first one was his grandfather who practiced surgery in Haleyville. Jonathan spent time with his grandfather and helped him with minor procedures. While in college, he was influenced by a family physician with whom he worked as they served the Boy Scouts in Huntsville.

Dr. Smith began college at Valley Forge Military College where he received the Associates in Science degree in 1991 and was valedictorian of his class. He graduated magma cum laude in 1993 from the University of Alabama at Huntsville with a degree in Biochemistry. He received the Doctor of Medicine degree from the University of South

Jonathan Smith, MD

Alabama in 1997 and completed a transitional internship and general surgery residency at William Beaumont Army Medical Center, El Paso, Texas, finishing training in 2002. He served on active duty in the US Army for 14 years. He was chief of general surgery prior to leaving his last duty station at Fort Campbell, Kentucky.

Dr. Smith is board certified in general surgery and is a fellow in the American College of Surgeons. He holds several awards and honors, including the Bronze Star Medal from Operation Iraqi Freedom and Meritorious Service Medal. His other awards include

- 2002 Resident Achievement Award, Society of Laparoendoscopic Surgeons.
- 1997 Alpha Omega Alpha (Medical Honor Society).
- 1997 Medical Alumni Leadership Award.
- 1996-97 USA College of Medicine Student Assembly President.
- 1996-97 Donna B. Lead Memorial Scholarship.
- 1993 Undergraduate Award in Analytical Chemistry.
- 1993 UAH Cross Country Leadership Award.
- 1993 Scholar Athlete Award.
- 1991 George C. Marshall Senior ROTC Award.
- 1990-91 Senior ROTC Cadet Battalion Commander, Valley Forge Military College.

Dr. Smith came to Fayette well experienced in surgery and developed a large surgical practice. His patients and the community admire and respect him greatly. Dr. Smith enjoys fishing and sailing in his brief free time.

Robert P. Bolling, MD, MPH

General Surgery, Plastic Surgery

Dr. Robert Bolling is a native of Fayette, Alabama, though he was born at Druid City Hospital in Tuscaloosa. His father owned a local pharmacy in Fayette. Dr. Breitling transferred his mother to DCH for a c-section. He was raised in Fayette and attended Fayette County High School, where he graduated in 1991. He was an outstanding athlete and played on the school's basketball team. He continued his education and played basketball at Bevill State Community College. Dr Breitling, his family doctor, greatly influenced him to attend medical school. Dr. Jon Sanford, a close personal friend of the family, was also instrumental in Dr. Bolling going to medical school.

Robert Bolling, MD, MPH

From Bevill State, Dr. Bolling went to Auburn University and graduated Summa Cum Laude with a BS degree in Chemistry in 1995. He then attended the University of Alabama School of Medicine. While in his third year of medical school, Dr. Bolling did a rotation with Dr. Garry Magouirk and spent some time with Dr. John Morrison. He graduated with the Medical Doctor degree and Master's of Public Health in 2000.

After medical school, Dr. Bolling went to the University of South Alabama College of Medicine where he completed a residency in general surgery in 2005. He then went to Tulane University School of Medicine for advanced training in plastic and reconstructive surgery.

In August of 2005, Dr. Bolling's training was interrupted due to hurricane Katrina. The hurricane greatly damaged Tulane and the medical school was closed for several months. Dr. Bolling came to Fayette and worked a few months until Tulane was back in order. He has maintained his medical privileges at Fayette Medical Center since that time. He returned to Tulane and completed the training in plastic and reconstructive surgery in 2007. He then went to Fairhope, Alabama and opened a private practice. He subsequently moved his practice to Fayette, where he is active in plastic and reconstructive surgery and general surgery.

He is board certified in plastic surgery and a member of the American Society of Plastic Surgeons.

When Dr. Bolling came to Fayette, he was well received in the community and quickly developed a large practice. He is a faithful member of Crossview Community Church in Fayette.

Medical Staff

The organizational meeting of the Fayette County Hospital Medical Staff was held on June 9, 1958, and from that time the Fayette hospital has always had an outstanding medical staff with exceptional skills and excellent credentials. Long before this meeting, Dr. McNease, Dr. Robertson, and Dr. Hodo had set a very high standard for quality of care. This commitment to high standards has been passed down and even enhanced over the generations. Pictured below is the 2006 Fayette Medical Center Medical Staff, representing only a few of the outstanding doctors who have practiced at Fayette.

Fayette Medical Center Medical Staff
Sitting L to R: Dr. Janice Hudson and Dr. Martha Jo Christian.
Standing L to R: Dr. Richard O. Rutland, Jr., Dr. Garry W.
Magouirk, Dr. Jon E. Sanford, Dr. Fred Yerby, Dr. Russell Sholl, Dr.
John E. Morrison, Dr. Charles W. Noland, Dr. Kenan Wannamaker,
and Dr. Gregory Stidham.

Fayette has always had an outstanding medical staff with exceptional leaders. Some examples follow. Dr. Benjamin McNease and Dr. Jon Sanford were presidents of the Medical Association of the State of Alabama (MASA). Dr. Banks Robertson and Dr. Henry Hodo were chief residents. Dr. Richard Rutland was *Good Housekeeping* Doctor of the Year. Dr. Garry Magouirk was president of the Alabama Academy of Family Physicians. Dr. John E. Morrison received several awards from medical societies including in 1998 the prestigious Kurt-Semm Award for Excellence in Pelviscopy by the American Association of Gynecologic Laparoscopists (AAGL).

Radiologists have been very important to Fayette Medical Center. Without them, Fayette would have not enjoyed the benefits of the most modern imaging technology locally. Starting in December 15, 1958, Dr. W. D. Anderson, radiologist and friend of Dr. McNease, began visiting the hospital each Thursday to read x-rays. Dr. Larkin Selman, a 1977 graduate of the University of Alabama School of Medicine, was Fayette's first full-time radiologist. He was followed by Ian Malcum and then by Dr. Neal Moss. Dr. Moss was greatly responsible for the large growth of the department from 1992 until 1999. With his expertise he made it financially feasible to purchase modern radiological equipment such as CT and MRI scanners. For a short time there was even an angiography room. Dr. Ron Phelps and Dr. John Kahler, radiologists affiliated with the Tuscaloosa group, were a great help in relieving Dr. Moss to allow him time off. When Dr. Moss left, the Tuscaloosa group started providing full-time coverage. They were aided by the installation of a system of teleradiology to transmit images to Tuscaloosa, thereby making it possible to provide the opinion of a radiologist on a 24-hour basis to the small community hospital.

Dr. Jonathan Smith and Dr. Robert Bolling, both surgeons, are the most recent additions to the medical staff. The role of surgeon may be the most crucial for the survival of a small hospital. Surgeons help family physicians to retain medical care locally that would otherwise be referred to urban centers. Also, the surgeon's craft makes use of intensive equipment and technical personnel that garner favorable reimbursement for the hospital, helping to assure its financial stability. Fayette has had the best of surgeons--Dr. Banks Robertson, Dr. Henry Hodo, Dr John Morrison, and currently, Dr. Jonathan Smith and Dr. Robert Bolling.

There were other doctors who came to Fayette and stayed for only a short time, but had some impact. Some examples are Dr. Paul Ashley, Dr. Rusty Bates, Dr. John Sea, Dr. Frank Evans, Dr. Peter Peacock, Dr. Phil Smith, Dr. William Davis, Dr. Neal Moss, Dr. Ron Phelps, Dr. Marby Garner, and Dr. John Kahler. These do not include doctors in residency who came thorough Fayette for practical experience as part of their training or for moonlighting.

The medical staff of Fayette Medical Center has evolved to keep up with the progression of medicine. The evolution has been guided in part by Fayette physicians' involvement in the leadership of professional associations and medical education that has produced a continuing supply of physicians. Thus, Fayette anticipates continued success with medical care through the sustained commitment to excellence that its health care leaders have pursued through both local and regional influence.

Administrators

Administrators have played an increasingly important role in Fayette's evolving health care system. Dating modern medicine in Fayette to Dr. McNease's arrival in 1926, the medical facilities remained under physician administration through the close attentions of Dr. McNease, Dr. Robertson, and Dr. Hodo. Dr. Robertson joined Dr. McNease in 1937, the same year that the McNease-Robertson Clinic-Hospital was built, and worked to gain this small hospital accreditation by the American College of Surgeons. He also became chairman of the Alabama Hospital Association in 1941-42. When Dr. Hodo opened surgical practice in Fayette in 1946, he took the role of administrator of the McNease-Robertson Hospital and held that position until the new hospital was built in 1958. With the new Fayette County Hospital/Fayette Medical Center and complications from regulations, technology, and payment systems, the medical community turned to professional, full-time administrators. These were Robert Boone, 1958-1980; Frank Wilbanks, 1980-1985; John Graves, 1985-1987; John Lucas, 1987-1990; Harold Reed, 1990-2008; and Barry Cochran 2008-2014; and Donald Jones2014-present.

Robert H. "Bob" Boone

The new Fayette County Hospital opened in September 24, 1958. Robert H. "Bob" Boone was hired as the first hospital administrator. He started early enough to monitor the hospital's construction. He was in this position for 20 years from 1958 until 1980. Bob and his wife, Trudy, were very happy living in Fayette. Trudy worked for a short while as the hospital infection control nurse.

Robert H. "Bob" Boone

Bob was very personable and a sportsman. He frequently took a break or had lunch with the employees. He loved Brunswick stew. He liked playing golf, and he and Dr. McNease often attended Ole Miss football games. He and some of the guys enjoyed shooting doves during season. He was sometimes made fun of because he was a terrible shot.

Bob was active in the Alabama Hospital Association, serving as its chairman, 1968-69. He was also chairman of the West Alabama Hospital Association. Bob was also was involved in the American Hospital Association and often attended its meetings. He was a long-time board member of Blue Cross and Blue Shield of Alabama.

Bob was involved in the local community. He was a member of the Exchange Club and Chamber of Commerce, which were the most active civic originations at that time.

As is sometimes required of administrators, Bob could be the "bad guy" in order to get the job done. At such times the employees felt intimidated, but he strived for what he thought was best for Fayette County Hospital and served the facility well. He guided the hospital and nursing home through several expansions and improvements from February 20, 1958 until July 23, 1980. Late in his career, Mr. Boone employed his first assistant administrator, Noel Hart, who worked five years in that capacity before taking the job of administrator in a Mississippi hospital. A few months later, Frank Wilbanks came on board as assistant administrator, and followed Bob as administrator when Bob retired shortly thereafter.

A. Frank Wilbanks

Frank was administrator for five years from 1980 until 1985. These were very difficult times for Fayette County Hospital and Nursing Home. Medicare was established in 1965 and hospitals were paid on a "retrospective cost-based reimbursement" system. Under this system of payment from 1967 until 1983, Medicare costs went up from $3 billion to $37 billion annually

The financial condition of the Fayette County Hospital and Nursing Home was highly stressed. Frank, in an attempt to help (with board approval), announced that all hourly employees would only work 72 hours per pay period and salaried employees would continue to work their 80 hours per pay period, but would only receive 72 hours pay. Frank was fair with his decision. The pay reduction applied to everyone, including himself. Most of the employees were upset but were supportive. This pay reduction continued for a few months, but no one resigned.

Due to these changes in Medicare, it became very difficult for small hospitals in Alabama to survive without an affiliation with a tertiary referral hospital. The hospital board decided that working with a large hospital should be considered. Proposals were sought from all interested parties and proposals were received from Druid City Hospital (DCH), Baptist Health System Birmingham, Caraway Methodist Hospital, and East Alabama Medical Center. A group of local citizens were appointed by the

Probate Judge and County Commission to evaluate the proposals.

Before the committee could evaluate the offers of agreement, the Probate Judge and County Commission entered a lease agreement with Baptist Heath System, whose representatives came to the hospital and took over operations. However, hospital board chairman T. C. Smith and board secretary William Thigpen sought the help of Attorney Bernard Harwood to file a restraining order in District Court. Attorney Harwood of the firm Rosen Harwood was very skilled--he was later appointed to the Alabama Supreme Court. The case was heard by the District Court to determine who had authority to enter a lease agreement on behalf of the hospital. Judge Cladus Junkin gave his ruling and stated,

> *By necessity, this Order has vested ownership of the Hospital in the Hospital Board, but that ownership is for control purposes alone and is in trust for the citizens of this county. The citizens of Fayette County are the true owners of the hospital regardless of who has control and that should not be forgotten by those in control.*

To stabilize the financial position of Fayette County Hospital and Nursing Home, on August 16, 1984, the board signed a management agreement with Druid City Hospital, but retained ownership of the facility.

Another management problem Frank faced was the

attempt of local United Auto Workers (UAW) Union, which was in the Arvin automotive plant, to also organize the hospital's nursing home and service employees. This created another few months of extreme stress. However, in the end and with the help of DCH and good legal counsel, the efforts of the UAW were unsuccessful.

When Frank was assistant administrator, in addition to his administrative duties, he was the purchasing agent. When he became administrator, he hired Frank Damico to replace him as purchasing agent, but he never filled the assistant administrator position. Frank Damico had a long experience in hospital supply sales and was excellent in his job.

Frank enjoyed living in Fayette. He had a swimming pool installed behind his house and enjoyed it very much. However, while mowing his lawn, he backed his lawn mower into his new pool. Frank Damico, who was an expert scuba diver, came to the rescue and helped Frank retrieve his lawn mower.

Fayette County Hospital and Nursing Home employees supported Frank as administrator during these difficult times. They understood the difficulties the facility was facing and wanted to do all they could do to help. Frank also maintained a good relationship the chairman of the board, Mr. T. C. Smith, and the entire hospital board. He had a good relationship with the medical staff, but they were not always in full agreement as to what action should be taken.

When the lease agreement was entered into with DCH, John Graves was employed as administrator of the hospital and Frank was moved to the position of administrator of the nursing home. A few months later, Frank resigned to start a business of his own in Fayette-- Spring Fresh Cleaners. The business was an immediate success. When he resigned, Mrs. Barbara Malcolm was named administrator of the nursing home.

John Graves

John Graves was administrator of Fayette County Hospital from 1985 to 1987. The first item of business for John was to change the image of the facility and develop a list of action items. He quickly gained the support of the department heads who helped create the action list. Among the items on the list were recruit doctors, especially a surgeon; adjust staffing to appropriate levels; and begin improvements to the facility.

John was not the most personable of administrators, but he got the job done. With recruitment he brought in Gordon King, MD, a general surgeon who only stayed about one year. He also recruited Rusty Bates, MD, an internist who remained almost four years. With the use of a consultant, John reduced staffing by about 18 full-time equivalent employees.

John immediately began making improvements in how the facility looked. The first recommendation from architects was to install a large triangular, unobstructed canopy for the front entrance. Some people loved the canopy and some people hated it, but they all talked about it. It made a statement that Fayette County Hospital was different. In addition to the canopy, a "V" shaped sign was built on the front lawn in front of the canopy with the DCH logo. Just behind the sign was a simple, but most important symbol: the United States flag on a 30-foot flag pole. With this change in image, there were also improvements made inside the hospital. One controversial item was carpet in all corridors and patient rooms. Nursing personnel could not be convinced that the carpet could be kept clean and, especially, sanitary. The first large construction project after the lease with DCH was in the north patient wing of the hospital. The project demolished the interior space and constructed a five-bed ICU and administrative suite.

One near disaster occurred when John employed as business manager Don Woodard, with whom he had previously worked. Don was very good in the business office, but when there was company party for the employees, Don dressed as a woman and played the part of "LaTonya." On this particular day everyone was in the cafeteria, and LaTonya tried just a little too hard to dance with Dr. Hodo. The next day, Don was back at his work in the business office, but LaTonya apparently left town and never returned.

John Graves and the medical staff could almost never agree. One reason for this was that when John first started to work as administrator, some of the doctors were delinquent with their medical records. John did not try to work with the doctors, but notified them that they were off staff until their records were up to date. This action was not well received, and one of the doctors never returned to the hospital.

When the lease with DCH was entered into, Fayette County hospital made a loan of several thousand dollars from DCH to fund the cost of structural changes to the facility. The operation of the hospital soon improved and the loan was repaid. However, during the time John was there, it was felt that he was a little too quick to make purchases. It was believed that some of John's superiors at DCH had the same thoughts. John was administrator for less than two years, then he became manager of the local Golden Eagle manufacturing plant. John Graves was followed by John Lucas.

John Lucas

John Lucas was administrator of Fayette County Hospital for three years, from 1987 until he retired in 1990. He had been the city manager of Demopolis, Alabama, which was Dr. Harold Breitling's home town. While in Demopolis, John had been a partner in and administrator of a nursing home. When John was in his early 50s, he and his wife Faye moved to Tuscaloosa so John could

John Lucas, Administrator (1987-90)

continue his education. After receiving the Bachelor of Science Degree from The University of Alabama, he went to the University of Alabama at Birmingham and arranged to do a residency in Health Administration with Jim Ford, Chief Executive Officer of Druid City Hospital. John said that after his residency Jim Ford asked him to stay on and become the night administrator. John asked Jim Ford, "What authority will I have?" and Jim Ford responded, "You are working in my place and you have the same authority as me." John was obviously a highly respected and competent administrator.

John left the position of assistant administrator of the Cancer Treatment Center in Tuscaloosa to take the administrator position at Fayette County Hospital.

John's greatest accomplishment while at Fayette was his first administrative decision-- the recruitment of the professional couple, John Morrison MD, general surgeon, and Janice Hudson MD, family physician. They practiced in the Fayette community for 20 years and made a tremendous contribution to the community and Fayette Medical Center. They continue to be missed greatly.

John Lucas was highly respected and honored by all employees. One of the reasons the employees were so fond of John is that in all of the years that John was administrator, he gave every employee a 6% pay adjustment at the end of each fiscal year. This amounted to an additional two-weeks' pay received each November.

John was very knowledgeable about the health care industry. He had a calm, reassuring demeanor, but he was not to be underestimated. He was well able to take a firm stand when needed. John was often referred to as a statesman.

John was active outside the community. He was chairman of the West Alabama Hospital Council, board member of the Alabama Hospital Association, served as a member and president of the Alabama Association of Healthcare Executives, was a member of the American College of Healthcare Professionals, and often attended the American Hospital Association meetings.

John and his wife, Faye, were very special people to both the hospital employees and the Fayette community. They were active in the First United Methodist Church of Fayette. John was an excellent mentor to Harold Reed and prepared him well to be the next administrator.

Harold Reed

(by John R. Wheat)

Harold Reed was born in Winfield, Alabama, about 18 miles north of Fayette and lived in the nearby area until moving to Fayette at the age of five. He went to Fayette County High School, graduating in 1967. He then attended Shelton Technical College in Tuscaloosa for two years and received an Associate Degree in Industrial Electricity. He began working at Fayette County Hospital and Nursing Home on April 3, 1970, as a maintenance engineer, which included the preventive

Harold Reed, Administrator
(1990-2008)

maintenance, upkeep, and repairs of all equipment, building, and grounds. Through the course of 38 years, his career progressed steadily as shown below:

- Maintenance Engineer (1970).
- Chief Engineer/Safety Officer.
- Director of Plant Operations, including departments of Engineering, House-keeping, and Laundry.
- Director of Facility Operations, adding to those departments above Dietary and Materials Management (1981).

- Assistant administrator, Fayette County Hospital and Nursing Home.
- Administrator of Perry County Hospital and Nursing Home, reopening the closed hospital and assuming operation of the nursing home (1989).
- Administrator, Fayette Medical Center (1990-2008).

During this advancement, he continued to attend school part-time. At Brewer State Community College, he earned the Associate in Arts degree; through The University of Alabama's New College, the Bachelor of Science in Administrative Sciences; and at UAB, a certificate in Health Services Administrative Development.

Harold Reed had worked with each of the professional administrators that served Fayette County Hospital and Nursing Home before him--Bob Boone, Frank Wilbanks, John Graves, and John Lucas. Under Mr. Boone, he was elevated to head of the Maintenance Department and assisted with day-to-day operations of the hospital, served as safety officer, and managed the logistical operations of the ambulance service. Even then, he had become involved in administration.

In 1981, Frank Wilbanks recognized Harold's continuing development and elevated him to director of facility operations. He served in this role over the next several years under Mr. Wilbanks and Mr. Graves. John Lucas made him assistant administrator, and Harold found Mr. Lucas to be an excellent mentor. Next, Harold was promoted within the Druid City Hospital management system to administrator and transferred to Perry County

Hospital and Nursing Home. His work in Perry County was valued highly. Subsequently, on January 1, 1990, he was transferred back to Fayette Medical Center to replace Mr. Lucas as administrator, a position he then held for 18 years.

During his administration, Harold led a $30 million construction and renovation program for the hospital. This included a new Dietary Department, a 21 bed expansion to the nursing home, a three-room expansion to surgery including central sterilization and supply; replacement of 45 patient rooms; a new eight-bed Intensive Care Unit; a remodeled hospital entrance and foyer with a Health Information Department, conference rooms and gift shop; and a new administrative suite and various small projects. Fayette County Hospital and Nursing Home gained national recognition for patient satisfaction under Harold's watch. Press Ganey, a nationally recognized leader in patient satisfaction surveys, found Fayette County Hospital to receive high survey scores and listed Fayette County Hospital among the top ten of Press Ganey facilities nationally based on its inpatient ratings.

Mr. Reed's professional activity expanded beyond hospital and county boundaries. He was a charter member of the E911 Board to facilitate the communication of emergency telephone calls in Fayette. He served as adjunct faculty of the University of Alabama College of Community Health Sciences from 1996 until 2008, assisting with teaching medical students and residents aspects of health care administration. As a charter member of the Rural Alabama Health Alliance (RAHA), he facilitated the inclusion of rural community voice in discussions of medical education and outreach. He was a member of the Alabama Rural Health Association and served as its president in 2006. He was a fellow in the College of Health Care Executives, a board member of the Alabama Hospital Association from 1996 until 2004, and member of the Blue Cross and Blue Shield Hospital Advisory Board for two terms, serving as chairman during the last term.

He has been active in community affairs, being a member of the Fayette Area Chamber of Commerce, including president in 1995; member of the President's Advisory Board of Bevill State Community College; board member of United Way of West Alabama; and member of Fayette Medical Center Foundation Board, Fayette Kiwanis Club, and Fayette County Extension Advisory Council. He is a member and has served as deacon of Unity Baptist Church. He remains a devoted husband and father.

Mr. Reed maintains a strong personal appreciation for the high quality care provided by the doctors and staff at Fayette Medical Center. In his words,

> *I am sure I would not still be alive if not for [Fayette physicians'] astute clinical acumen, up-to-date expertise, and connectedness to some of the world's most advanced medical experts. On the evening of March 22, 1995, when I was in a meeting with a few of doctors, I collapsed with a cerebral aneurism that was*

located in a very critical part of the brain. This would have resulted in my immediate death had it not been for our modern CT scanner, the well trained radiologist, and the expertise of our medical staff, who knew the care that was needed to prevent my brain from swelling and who engaged immediate emergency medical transportation. All of these factors contributed to my survival to reach Dr. Evan Zeiger, a world renowned neurosurgeon, who without doubt performed life-saving surgery for me. This proves the benefit of high quality medical care in rural areas, including such advances as CT, MRI, and ultrasound as a standard of care that should be readily available.

When Harold first became administrator for Fayette Medical Center, he employed Luke Standeffer as assistant administrator. Luke had recently graduated from The University of Alabama with a degree in Health Administration. While employed at Fayette Medical Center, Luke continued his education and received the Master in Business Administration degree. Luke proved to be very bright and was a great help to Harold in his early years as administrator. Luke was especially valuable during the time of Harold's illness, as described above. Harold was out of work for almost two months, during which time Luke served as acting administrator. Luke was employed at Fayette for seven years before taking a position with Health South as an administrator. He subsequently returned to DCH Health System and now is the executive vice present and administrator of Northport Medical Center.

Late in Mr. Reed's tenure as administrator, Tom Hood was employed as assistant administrator. However, Tom had accepted a position as administrator of a hospital in Mississippi shortly before Harold's announced retirement, so Barry Cochran came to work as the administrator in 2007.

Barry S. Cochran

Barry Cochran came to work at Fayette Medical Center as administrator in June of 2007. He came with broad knowledge and experience in health care. He started his career as director of pharmacy at Baptist Cherokee Hospital in Centre, Alabama. Within a few years he was promoted to administrator, and after only a few more years he became the concurrent president of Baptist Cherokee in Centre and Baptist DeKalb Hospital in Fort Payne, Alabama. He later served as CEO in various small and large hospitals.

Mr. Cochran's administration began in parallel with a national depression that has had significant effects on rural economies, including health care. Jeff Huff, who came on board as chief financial officer just prior to Mr. Cochran's arrival, has worked with Barry to address issues affecting the financial viability of the hospital. Perhaps foremost among these issues was the departure of surgeon John

Barry Cochran,
Administrator (2007-)

Morrison and family physician Janice Hudson a few months after Barry started to work. They had finally given in to recruitment efforts from their alma mater, Louisiana State University, to get Dr. Morrison back home as a medical teacher and administrator. Their departure greatly exacerbated the hospital's financial stress. However, Mr. Cochran soon recruited Dr. Jonathan Smith, a general surgeon, and Dr. Robert Bolling, a plastic surgeon, to practice at Fayette Medical Center.

Other stressors included the retirement of Dr. Rutland from part-time practice in the nursing home. He was replaced through a contract company that provided Dr. Dick Owens to be the on-site physician. Also, Barry promoted Michelle Robertson, RN to be the nursing home administrator.

As did those before him, Barry maintains many professional and community affiliations and has been recognized for his professional service. For example, he is a fellow in the American College of Healthcare Executives and is past-president of the Alabama Hospital Association. He received the Gold Medal of Excellence award, which is the highest award given by the Alabama Hospital Association.

During Barry's short tenure at Fayette Medical Center, he has proven himself an excellent administrator and has gained the respect of the employees. Even as many small rural hospitals are facing uncertain futures, given the financial distress that appears to be compounded by evolving federal health policies, Fayette continues to expect state-of-the-art medical care under the guidance of Mr. Cochran and at the hands of its beloved physicians.

Employees of Fayette County Hospital and Medical Center

Many dedicated and loyal employees have worked or continue to work at Fayette Medical Center. Some of these began their careers in the old clinic-hospital downtown or in the Fayette County Hospital and Nursing Home.

Blanche Whitley, as director of nurses, is one of the first to come to mind as a loyal and dedicated employee. Flossie Kizzire worked alongside Blanche at the old hospital downtown and also at the new Fayette County Hospital. Flossie was assistant director of nurses for a time. When Blanche retired, she was followed as director of nurses by Dot Bobo. The next director was Mae Davis, then Pam Farris, and finally Kathy Griffith who continues to hold the position today. Kathy Griffith is a self-professed workaholic with 27 years of service. She started her career as an obstetrics nurse and through extreme dedication and commitment grew in her position to become assistant administrator and chief nursing officer. She demonstrates outstanding leadership skills and superior ability to interpret and apply accreditation standards. Kathy's abilities have been reflected in outstanding surveys by the JCAHO. She is an exceptional person and also serves as associate pastor for the First Methodist Church of Fayette.

Wanda Moore has 37 years of service, starting as a ward clerk and progressing to her present station as administrative secretary for Kathy Griffith.

Sally Cash worked 33 years; several were in a part-time capacity and served in many nursing positions. At one time she was Assistant Director of Nursing but most recently she has been Director of Education.

Annie Shackelford was the first African American registered nurse to be employed at Fayette County Hospital and was a long-time ICU nurse.

Phoebe Kizzire had the reputation as the best surgical aide that ever worked at Fayette Medical Center.

Arlene Berry has been employed as a nurse and nursing supervisor for 18 years. She is currently a supporter and mentor to her sister, Theresa Berry, who also worked at FMC for a time and now is in medical school. After completion she hopes to practice in Fayette.

Rena Nalls has worked 19 years as an evening shift nurse and nursing supervisor.

Teresa Riley has worked in the hospital and Nursing Homes and has been an LPN and RN during 21 years of service.

Wanda Cannon worked for 38 years, most of which was in the Emergency Department with several years as Director of ED.

Youonia Stocks worked 27 years as a nurse and nursing supervisor. Then she completed her career with several years as Infection Control Nurse and employee health nurse.

Belinda Davis has been employed for 36 years. Most of those years was as an outstanding Emergency Department nurse.

Earnie Bonner was a remarkable nurse for 22 years. Starting as an LPN in the nursing home, she transferred to the hospital and worked in all nursing areas. During that time, she returned to school and was able to complete the last 11 years of service as an RN.

Betty Whitley retired with 33 years of service. She started to work as a nursing assistant, became an LPN, and then progressed to RN. During her career, she developed the Infection Control Department and built the quality assurance program through all its phases.

Jettie Wilson, an LPN with 33 years of service, worked in all areas of nursing.

Barry Eads, an employee of 36 years, came to work as an LPN and soon afterwards became an EMT paramedic. His name became synonymous with the ambulance service. After receiving his Bachelor in Science in Nursing he was promoted to the director of Inpatient Care and Emergency Department. After additional studies, he obtained his Masters in Health Administration. He became an assistant administrator before his retirement. Barry went on to hold positions of director of the Emergency Department and director of nursing at two other facilities.

Kim Jordan, director of respiratory care, built an

outstanding Respiratory Care Department over a long, successful career.

Jackie Waldon, with 21 years, started in physician recruitment and built the Communications and Marketing Department. She is known for excellence in writing and advertising. She is also known for starting the foundation.

Centhia Melton for 15 years has worked as secretary to the Administrator and has done an excellent job as Medical Staff Coordinator.

Sheryl Lynn and Wanda Bonner came to work at the same time 21 years ago. At this time there was an opening at Human Rescores and at Home Health. They both applied for both positions. Sheryl went to Human Rescores and Wanda to Home Health. Both have stayed in their original departments until today.

Barbara Malcom, with 25 years of service, began work as an LPN and proved to be an outstanding emergency room nurse. She continued her career by becoming an RN. She worked in case management until she was promoted to director of nursing in the nursing home. From there she was soon promoted to administrator of the nursing home. Other administrators who came before her were Bob Boone and Frank Willbanks. Those who followed her as nursing home administrator were Harold Reed, JoAnn Nichols, and Michelle Robertson.

Deloris Thompson was the first registered nurse to work in the nursing home and was a long-term employee there.

Nan Glassglow, a Registered Nurse, was a long-time, exceptional worker in the hospital and nursing home.

Linda Mitchell worked for a total of 38 years as an LPN in faithful care of nursing home patients.

Mary Ham, in 28 years of service, has been a medical-surgical nurse, ICU nurse, and hospital house supervisor. She now works in long term care as a supervisor.

Linda Powell, with 42 years of service, started as a ward clerk and progressed to administrative secretary working for the nursing home administrator.

In recent years, the long term care staff has done an excellent job under the guidance of Michelle Robertson, long term care administrator with 21 years of service; Andrea Johnson, director of nursing with 21 years of service; and supervisors Mary Ham and Nan Glassglow (25 years of service each), Wanda Brown (14 years of service), and Susan Taylor (22 years of service). Their compliance with licensure and certification standards produced numerous deficiency-free surveys by the Department of Public Health.

Gertrude Stanford, the first food service manager, was an excellent manager and known for her big heart. She was followed by Nancy Maddox who did an outstanding job for 20 years before moving to the Department of Public Health. Odessa Walker, long-time dietary employee and excellent cook, also served as food service manager.

Lynnwood Christian and Doug Berry worked in both the lab and x-ray departments, covering untold nights of call and providing excellent quality x-ray and lab results until 1975, when Gaillard Stoker came to work as the first officially trained radiology technician. Susanne McGraw worked in the laboratory and x-ray and helped Gaillard take radiology call.

Dee Barger, member of the American Society of Clinical Pathologists, was a long-time, faithful employee in the lab.

Bill Durr followed Gaillard as head of the Radiology Department and he was followed by Sandy Hester, Pat Connell, Bill Fikes, then June Keith, Jeff Madison, Anthony Mosley, and John Files, who works in the position today. John has built an excellent department, both in quality and efficiency. He has arranged for all technicians to be cross-trained in multiple disciplines. John, with 19 years of service, has also built a department of long tenured personnel which includes Mickey Brewer (23 years), Shannon Jones (20 years), Cindy Files (20 years), and Christy Nelson (13 years). Cheryl Farris with 22 years and Tanya Damico with 24 years both work in ultrasound.

Lynnwood Christian, who enjoyed being a prankster himself, had to stay on his guard. One instance occurred when administrator Bob Boone was away from the facility, but was expected to return later in the day. At lunch time, Lynnwood came through the cafeteria in his usual jovial mood on his way to the serving line. As he passed by the window, he noticed with alarm that his red pickup truck had been pushed over into Bob Boone's private parking place! Everyone had a good laugh as a confused, angry, and a little bit anxious Lynwood scurried to move his truck before Bob, who could be the bad guy, returned. Another episode of good humor occurred one day when several of the guys who regularly hunted with Bob were sitting with him in the cafeteria. Bob loved to dove hunt and considered himself a good shot. However, he often shot at birds that were too far away, but everyone was afraid to tell him. This day Bob looked out the window and said "Gaillard, when you have a shot at a dove about where the corner of the building is, how much you lead them?" Without thinking, Gaillard replied, "At that distance I wouldn't take a shot; it's too far away!" Everyone had a big laugh, though Bob never understood why, and Gaillard was relieved when the moment passed.

Lynnwood was not just a prankster, but was an excellent employee. The facility often had an employee of the month and quarter, but only once did it name an employee of the year. Lynwood was elected to this well-deserved position by all the employees.

Lawson White, the first maintenance engineer, was extremely dedicated and committed to the facility.

James Burkhalter worked with Lawson White as one of the first maintenance engineers with 40 years of service, he also had extreme dedication. He came to work anytime he was called, whether on call or not. He had the reputation that he could fix anything. Due to James's leadership all employees in the Maintenance Department had long tenure. These employees include Phillip Cannon (28 years), Jimmy Dean (20 years), Jonathan Burkhalter (17 years), and James Cotton (15 years).

Della Mitchum, the first director of housekeeping, did an excellent job. Frances Driver was an exceptional environmental services worker, also. Ronnie Wilson worked in environmental services and was one of the best, if not the best, floor finisher ever to work at Fayette Medical Center.

Lillian Watkins, the first director of laundry, was a diligent worker. She was followed in this position by her daughter, Eulene Barnett, who was also a very dedicated worker. Eulene's daughter, Sally Ham, worked in the Physical Therapy Department as a secretary.

Larry Watkins started to work as a clerk in general storage and after going to school to become a registered nurse, he transferred to surgery and soon became the director of surgery. He later returned to general storage as the director of material management.

Katie Black was the first director of medical records. Pam Stocks followed Katie with 35 years of service in medical records and is now director of health information management. Cindy Renfroe has been a coworker of Pam's for 35 years and is an excellent coder and transcriptionist.

Diane White began directly out of high school and through 42 years of service has successfully worked in every position in the business office. Other business office employees with long, outstanding records were Mary Smith, the first manager of the office; Terrell Jones, the first comptroller; Tommie Shelton in payroll; Sheila Swendial in billing; Susan Hones in long term care billing; and receptionists Mary Smith and Florence Farris.

Tina Gilliam, patient admission coordinator, has worked untiringly for 35 years and has worked whenever needed to get this important job done.

With each passing generation, the faithful employees

of the Fayette health care facilities have been constant in helping provide the people of Fayette County and the surrounding area with exceptional care. I am sure I have failed to mention many other dedicated and loyal employees, all of whom should be recognized for their service to the community.

Significant happenings in the history of Fayette County Medicine:

- December 14, 1819--Alabama became a state.
- June, 1842--Fayette became a county.
- 1800-1859--Pioneer doctor, irregular doctors, and doctors without formal training were prevalent in the practice of medicine.
- June 24, 1926--Dr. B. W. McNease came to Fayette.
- 1926--Fayette County had its first paved road.
- 1929--Flu epidemic came into Fayette.
- 1929--30 Great Depression started.
- April 1, 1936--Dr. McNease paid $500 for land to build clinic.
- 1937--Clinic construction complete at a cost of $11,000.
- 1937--Dr. John Banks Robertson, Sr., a surgeon, came to Fayette.
- 1938--McNease-Robertson Hospital was built.
- 1939 to 1945--World War II in process.
- 1941 to 1942--Dr. Robertson was president of the Alabama Hospital Association.
- 1941 to1945--Inez Fowler, after completing studies, started working at Fayette as lab tech.
- 1947--Dr. Robertson retired due to stress of work causing health concerns.

- 1947--Dr. Henry Gunter Hodo, Jr., a surgeon, came to Fayette.
- 1950 to1953--Korean War.
- 1952--Dr. Inez Fowler, after medical school internship and time with Red Cross, began medical practice in Fayette.
- 1954—Four mill tax for new Fayette County Hospital approved by county vote.
- August, 1954--Dr. Richard Rutland started his practice in Fayette.
- February 20, 1958--Robert Boone became administrator.
- September 21, 1958--Grand opening of Fayette County Hospital.
- September 24, 1958--McNease-Hodo Hospital closed.
- September 24, 1958--Fayette County Hospital officially opened as a 35-bed hospital with four patients; semi-private rooms were $10/day, private rooms $17/day.
- December 15, 1958--W. D. Anderson, radiologist and friend of Dr. McNease, began visiting the hospital each Thursday and reading x-rays.
- 1959--Dr. Harold E. Breitling began his practice in Fayette.
- Early years of FCH--Lab employees did X-rays as well as performing lab procedures.
- 1962--Addition of a 38-bed nursing home.
- April 27, 1964--Tuscaloosa Pathology started a referral and consulting lab.

- November 23, 1965--Nursing home expansion of 22 beds, bringing total beds to 60.
- 1966--Unit secretaries added to assist nursing service, but only on first and second shifts.
- July 1, 1966--Hospital approved to participate in Medicare program.
- March 27, 1967--Addition of 26 beds, second nursing station, and OB patient wing open to the public, increasing hospital capacity to total of 61 beds.
- October 16, 1968--Administrator salary increased to $17,440 per year.
- 1968--Administrator Robert Boone was chairman of the Alabama Hospital Association.
- May 24, 1971--Board requested a traffic light at entrance to hospital and entrance was changed to Side Street.
- September 27, 1971--The hospital average daily census was 48.4 with 61 total beds.
- March 6, 1972--Mrs. Blanche Whitley, director of nursing was awarded "Woman of the Year" by Exchange Club.
- 1972--Dr. Jon Sanford moved his practice from Gordo to Fayette.
- May 26, 1973--The hospital assumed operation of the ambulance service that was previously run by Howell Funeral Home.
- 1973--Dr. Inez Fowler, after further training, started psychiatry practice in Fayette.

- July 22, 1974--Two x-ray technicians became available on a full time basis.
- February 24, 1975--Fayette's first registered pharmacist, Pat McCrackin, was employed three days per week, moving to full-time in May.
- April 24, 1977--The Exchange Club credited Dr. B. W. McNease for implementing"modern" medicine in Fayette County.
- April 24, 1977--Nursing home was renovated and 51-bed wing was added bringing total to 101 beds.
- June 26, 1977--Hospital began offering respiratory therapy service via contract with by Larry Andrews, LLC.
- July 5, 1978--Nurse Midwife Lovie Oswalt delivered her last baby.
- 1979--McNease-Hodo Clinic downtown was closed.
- 1979--New McNease-Hodo Clinic was opened, and Dr. Hodo honored for his great contributions to medicine in Fayette.
- 1979--Frank Wilbanks became administrator.
- 1983--Dr. Magouirk started practice in Berry.
- August 16, 1984--DCH Health Care Authority leased Fayette County Hospital and Nursing Home for 20 years, until August 11, 2016.
- 1984--Allen Blackwell, VP of DCH, was named interim administrator at FCH.
- 1984--There were 230 employees and 28 total medical staff members, including part time subspecialist from Tuscaloosa. Active staff were

Dr. Richard Rutland, Dr. Phil Smith, Dr. Harold Breitling, Dr. Henry Hodo, Dr. Peter Peacock, Dr. Jon Sanford, Dr. Roger Moss, Dr. Garry Magouirk, and Dr. Chandrin.

- 1984--John Graves became administrator of hospital.
- 1984--Frank Wilbanks was transferred to Administrator of nursing home.
- 1985--Hospital gained a new diagnostic nuclear medicine department, mammographic machine, and x-ray machine.
- 1986--Dr. Magouirk moved practice to Fayette.
- 1986--Barbara Malcom was named administrator of nursing home.
- 1986--Lynnwood Christian was named employee of the year.
- 1986--Renovation of north wing of hospital with a 5-bed ICU and administrative suite and renovation of front lobby.
- 1986--Combined nurses station one and two to be a central nurses station.
- 1986--Laundry closed and service contracted to DCH, medical records moved from trailer into laundry space, administrator moved from trailer to new administrative suite in hospital.
- 1986--Fayette County Hospital Foundation chartered.
- 1986--Pam Farris RN, CCRN named director of nursing.
- 1987--John Lucas became administrator.

- 1987--Millport Clinic open with a physician.
- June 1987--Dr. John E. Morrison and Dr. Janice L. Hudson started practice in Fayette.
- 1988--CT suite constructed, making Fayette one of the state's first rural hospitals to install a CT scanner.
- 1990--Harold Reed became administrator.
- 1990--Kathy Griffith became director of nursing, assistant administrator of nursing, and chief nursing officer.
- 1991--Laparoscopic surgery was begun by Dr. Morrison.
- 1992--Dr.Fred Yerby started practice in Fayette.
- 1992--Home Health Agency was established.
- 1992 to 2000--C. Neil Moss, MD became full-time radiologist.
- 1993--Rezwan Islam, MD established practice at Millport Clinic.
- 1993--Mobile MRI service was started.
- 1993--Physical therapy expanded into the old ambulance house.
- 1994--Heliport and new parking lot were constructed.
- 1994--DCH opened dialysis clinic in Fayette.
- 1994--Construction of 21-bed nursing home wing and new kitchen funded by FCH Board.
- 1999--Expansion in preparation for new nursing wing.
- 1994--Dr. Van Johnson began cataract surgery.
- 1994--Meditech computer linkage installed.

- 1994--Dr. Grubbs left after four years as full-time ER physician. Hospital went to contracted Emergency Department service.
- 1995--Hospice and durable medical equipment service were started; Dr. Volker Jacobs, German physician, began working with Dr. Morrison doing research; Dr. Luis Pernia began performing endoscopic carpal tunnel procedures; and a new larger surgical suite was built.
- August 8, 1996--The DCH lease was extended for 20 years, until August 31, 2016.
- 1996--Outpatient Clinic constructed from the old kitchen.
- 1996--Hospice and durable medical qquipment were expanded and relocated to Fayette Square Shopping Center.
- 1996--Radiology began doing angiography procedures.
- 1996--Fayette County Hospital and Nursing Home were renamed Fayette Medical Center.
- 1997--Teleradiology equipment was installed, connected to DCH.
- 1997--New central sterile Supply Department was built adjoining surgery and a new surgical wing was named after Dr. Henry G. Hodo, Jr.
- 1998--Fayette Medical Center celebrated its 40th Anniversary.
- 1999--A new mechanical building was constructed; expansion prepared for a new nursing wing; a wing of new patient rooms was opened; cardiac rehab

was initiated; and Dr. Martha Jo Christian started practice in Fayette.

• 2000--Dr. Lisolette Métier, a German gynecological surgeon, traveled from Germany to Fayette Medical Center to have gall bladder and hernia repair done laparoscopically by Dr. Morrison.

• 2000--Telesurgery equipment was used to broadcast surgery procedure by Dr. Morrison to fourteen physicians in Miami, FL.

• 2000--A new MRI (fixed base) was installed at FMC to replace the old mobile MRI.

• 2000--Balanced Budget Act began with large Medicare cuts for hospital.

• 2001--Construction completed on new hospital front entrance, business office, medical records, gift shop, and lobby, chapel, and conference rooms.

• 2001--NKase, new clot dissolving drug, became available at FMC.

• 2002--FCH Board renovated long term care station two with new call system and corridors.

• 2003--Long term care "step-it-up" program was begun in August; Employer of Choice Award was given to FMC in November.

• 2004--FMC was given the "Above and Beyond" award for its support of the Alabama National Guard and Reserve.

• 2005--New hospital administrative suite area was constructed just off front lobby; FMC purchased a 16-slice GE Pro Light-Speed CT scanner.

- 2006--FMC received employee satisfaction award from Sperduto & Associates for "Commitment and Excellence in Employee Satisfaction Measurement."
- 2007--FMC awarded by Sperduto & Associates for "Greatest Increase in Employee Satisfaction;" the Pharmacy was renovated and relocated to surgery hall; JoAnn Nichols, RN became administrator of long term care; Barry Cochran became administrator; and on October 1, 2007, the DCH lease was extended until September 30, 2016.
- October 31, 2008--Fayette County Home Care was transferred to LHC Group.
- September 2008--Ambulance service was transferred to North Star Ambulance Service.
- January 1, 2012--Hospice of FMC joined with Hospice of West Alabama.
- November 2007--Dr. John E. Morrison and Dr. Janice Hudson moved back to Louisiana to teach at LSU, their alma mater.
- 2008--Richard Rutland, MD retired after fifty-four years of service to FMC; the Emergency Department was renovated.
- July 25, 2013--Michelle Robertson, RN became administrator of long term care.

Epilogue by William A. Curry, MD

Being a physician can be a lonely business. Even though practicing medicine re-quires establishing rela-tionships with patients and families, taking histories, making physical examina-tions, and recommending plans of investigation and treatment, the responsi-bil-ities and the complexi-ties of decision-making can leave the physician longing for help. Often that can come only from a colleague who has been there, too—someone who not only can

William A. Curry, MD is Professor of Medicine and Associate Dean of Rural and Primary Care at UAB School of Medicine

understand the personal and social stresses of medical practice, but who also can contribute to the problem-solv-ing that is the mark of good diagnosis and treatment. Much of our best work is done in collaboration.

When Dr. Benjamin Wilberne McNease arrived in Fayette in 1926, he was only a generation removed from a time when most physicians in the rural South practiced medicine part-time, combining it with farming, teaching, ministry, or other work. The change involved much more than hours on the job, however. The early 1900s marked a shift from medical practice based on observation, experience, and apprenticeship to a standard of scientific evidence and an academic model of rigorous education and training like that Dr. McNease pursued.

So it was not surprising that Dr. McNease, with his academic preparation as a student and as a professor, would establish not only a clinic but a hospital, a place where physicians could work in collaboration. Besides serving the medical needs of the people of Fayette County and the surrounding region, it became a focal point for a medical group that supported and complemented each other. Over the years, the Fayette medical community has earned the respect of Alabama physicians for clinical excellence, professionalism, and civic responsibility. The concept of community medicine embodied in the work of Drs. William Willard and David Mathews was well established in Fayette fifty years before it gained academic structure through the University of Alabama College of Community Health Sciences.

My own exposure to the work and role models of Fayette medicine started early. The first intravenous line I ever saw was attached to my grandfather while he was an overnight patient in the McNease–Robertson Hospital. I remember Dr. McNease as a powerful and imposing figure. Later, when my grandfather needed a home visit, it was their dashing young colleague, Dr. Dick Rutland, who came to nearby Kennedy–giving me the memorable experience of his inspiring and comforting presence that is described earlier in this book. I wanted to be like him.

When the time for my application to medical school approached, I spent time with Dr. Jon Sanford, then practicing in Gordo, to make rounds at the North Pickens County Hospital. My own family physician and role model, Dr. William Hill, wanted me to get to know this young, dynamic doctor. From their perspective on medicine and community, I felt well oriented and recommended to the profession I hoped to enter. When my other beloved grandfather fell seriously ill, it was Dr. Sanford who made a home visit in Carrollton while covering in Dr. Hill's absence. Once again I could see the comfort and peace that a family can receive from a competent and caring physician. Jon, soon after that, moved to Fayette, and our friendship continues to this day.

All this would be more than enough gifts to me from the physicians and health care community of Fayette, and their contributions to patients and community would be noteworthy and deserving of the commemoration of this and other records. However, the relationship of Fayette physicians–particularly Dr. Rutland–with the University of Alabama College of Community Health Sciences adds another layer of historic accomplishment. By the 1970s, it was unusual for academic medical programs to bring practicing rural physicians onto their faculty–especially in leadership positions. But that was exactly what Bill Willard, David Mathews, and John Burnum did in tapping Dick Rutland to lead the new family medicine residency in Tuscaloosa. Not only did Dr. Rutland help establish what has become one of the nation's most successful family practice programs, he created a lifeline for future physicians to the Fayette medical community. As a site for medical student and resident teaching, Fayette has been a natural attraction for the young physicians who have chosen it as their own practice home.

The story of this book comes full circle now, with Dr. McNease's great vision being fulfilled through the University of Alabama College of Community Health Sciences, the successor to the medical school where he taught in Tuscaloosa, bringing physicians in training to learn and be enriched by the legacy of the McNease–Hodo Clinic, the hospital, and medical staffs yet to be formed. My own story also comes full circle. Dr. Rutland's groundbreaking work in Tuscaloosa made it easier for another rural physician to find work there–for me it was first as chair of the internal medicine and later as dean of CCHS. My debt to Dr. Rutland, Dr. Sanford, Dr. McNease, Dr. Hodo, and to our younger colleagues including Dr. Garry Magouirk can be repaid only by passing on to others what was so freely given to me. It can be a lonely business, but the practice of medicine also can be a place of the richest and most rewarding professional relationships. We all can be grateful that medicine has been graced by visionary and committed leaders who answer a call to more than routine work, who insist on solutions to the problems their patients face – whether they are scientific or social, administrative or personal. The fruits of their labors are better ways of practicing medicine and of being physicians–practices well-served and lives well-lived. It is an honor to be their colleague.

Acknowledgments

If you find a turtle sitting on a fence post, you know he had a lot of help in getting there. I feel like this turtle because I have had help from so many in this project. I would like to start by saying how grateful I am to my lovely wife, Kathy, for her encouragement and patience through this project. Others to be acknowledged are shown below.

Dr. Richard O. Rutland, Jr. helped grow the idea of this book and assisted in so many ways including editing and contributing much of the information. Mrs. Nancy Rutland also contributed details. Mrs. Nancy, Mrs. Melissa McFall Rutland, and Dr. Rutland helped to develop Dr. Rutland's chapter.

Dr. John R. Wheat helped to make this book possible by his collaboration and his professional input. He was gracious enough to write the "Foreword." Also, Dr. Wheat was a great help as senior editor.

Dr. William A. Curry provided an excellent "Epilogue," capturing the spirit.

Mr. Delbert Reed was very helpful with his contributions and editing.

Each of the following were extremely helpful in collecting information for their individual chapters—Dr. Harold Breitling, Dr. Jon Sanford (with the assistance of Mrs. Mary Anne Sanford), Dr. Garry Magouirk, Dr.

John Morrison and Dr. Janice Hudson, Dr. Charles Nolen, Dr. Fred Yerby, Dr. Martha Jo Christian, Dr. Gregory Stidham, Dr. Jonathan Smith, and Dr. Robert Bolling.

Mr. Joe McCrakin assisted with the chapter on Dr. McNease, and Mr John Banks Robertson, Jr. assisted with the Dr. Robertson, Sr. chapter.

Dr. Patricia Norton was great help as Copy Editor.

Those listed below, and others that I may have overlooked, have helped in many ways.

Mr. and Mrs. Horace Berry

Mr. Phillip Clark

Mr. Barry Cochran

Mr. Barry Eads

Mrs. Cynthia Melton

Mr. Bill Hardekopf

Mr. Richard Nelson

Mrs. Danylu Nichols

Mr. Tommy Norwood

Mrs. Beverly Robertson

Mr. Bill Robertson

Mr. Gaillard Stoker

Mr. Reedus Wheat

Fayette County Library

The Historical Society

Mrs. Jackie Waldon

Nichols Studio

Drawing by Becky Wright

McNease Robertson Hodo Clinic Hospital

Fayette Medical Center

**Every effort has been made to ensure the accuracy of this document although some errors may exist.

Index

American Academy of Family Physicians 35, 40, 87, 99, 105
American Association of Gynecologic Laparoscopists 94, 112
American College of Healthcare Executives 134
American College of Healthcare Professionals 126
American College of Legal Medicine 97
American College of Surgeons 12, 14, 15, 20, 60, 61, 108, 115
American Hospital Association 117, 126
American Medical Association 5, 44, 50, 97
American Society of Clinical Pathologists 140
American Society of Plastic Surgeons 110
Anderson, W. D. 112, 145
Andrews, Larry 147
Ashley, Paul, 113
Babb (Rutland), Nancy 30, 32
Bailey, Lester 57
Barger, Dee 140
Barnett, Eulene 142
Bates, Rusty 113, 122
Berry, Arlene 136
Berry, Doug 139
Berry, Harold xvi
Berry, Horace xvi, 158
Berry, Theresa 136
Black, Katie 142
Black, Mavis 58
Blackwell, Allen 147
Blakeney, A. Lanthus xv, xvi
Blue Cross Blue Shield of Alabama 20, 24, 117, 130
Bobo, Arlington Henry 41
Bobo, Dot 135

Bolling, Robert P. 109, 110, 113, 134, 158
Bonner, Earnie 137
Bonner, Wanda 138
Boone, Robert H. "Bob" 65, 74, 115, 116, 117, 128, 138, 140, 145. 146
Brand, Rocky 58
Brandon, A.C. xvi
Brandon, Edna xvi
Brandon, J. A. xvi
Brandon, Jim Walker xvi
Breitling, Harold E. 26, 37, 41, 42, 43, 44, 45, 58, 96, 97, 98, 109, 125, 145, 148, 157
Brewer, Mickey 140
Brock (Hodo), Naomi 18, 21
Brown, Robert W. 31
Brown, Wanda 139
Burkhalter, James 141
Burkhalter, Jonathan 141
Cannon, Phillip 141
Cannon, Wanda 136
Carter, Richard xvii
Cash, Sally 136
Chambless, Rose Ann 58
Christian, Lynnwood 101, 139, 140, 148, 151
Christian, Martha Jo 101, 102, 103, 111, 158
Civil War xv, 45
Clemons, Wiley 14, 57
Clemons, Florence 57
Clinics
    The McNease Clinic 6, 44, 46, 61
    McNease-Hodo Clinic 20, 35, 44, 46, 53, 66, 72, 73, 86, 147, 156
    Northwest Alabama Mental Health Center 27
Cochran, Barry S. 74, 115, 132, 133, 134, 152, 158